Mrs H. M. Mills
514 Broad Ave
Albany, Ga.

Studies in Luke's Gospel

STUDIES IN
LUKE'S GOSPEL

By

FRANK STAGG

Convention Press

NASHVILLE   TENNESSEE

Code Number: Church Study Course
This book is number 32 in category 2, section
for Adults and Young People

Library of Congress catalog card number: 67-14440

Printed in the United States of America

430. JE 67 R.R.D.

Dedicated

to

M. E. Williamson

under whose

understanding and concerned pastoral ministry

a lad from South Louisiana

found

the sense of direction

which turned him to

the gospel ministry

About the Author

FRANK STAGG was born in Eunice, Louisiana. In 1934 he graduated from Louisiana College with a B.A. degree. He received the Th.M. degree in 1938 from Southern Baptist Theological Seminary, and in 1943, the Ph.D. from the same seminary.

Later Dr. Stagg spent one year (1953–54) in study in the University of Edinburgh, Scotland, and the University of Basel, Switzerland. In 1955, Louisiana College conferred on him the LL.D. degree.

From 1941–44, Dr. Stagg served as pastor of First Baptist Church, DeRidder, Louisiana. From 1945–64, he taught at New Orleans Baptist Theological Seminary as professor of New Testament and Greek and chairman of the Graduate Council in the School of Theology. He is now James Buchanan Harrison professor of New Testament Interpretation at Southern Baptist Theological Seminary.

Dr. Stagg is the author of *The Book of Acts, The Early Struggle for an Unhindered Gospel; New Testament Theology;* and *Exploring the New Testament.*

With his wife (Evelyn Owen) and his children, Ted, Bobby, and Ginger, Dr. Stagg traveled in Europe and the Mediterranean countries during 1953–54. His hobbies are boating, hunting, and fishing. In the summer of 1967, Dr. Stagg and his family again traveled in Europe before he began a year's leave to study in Germany on a grant from the American Association of Theological Schools.

Contents

Church Study Course

THE CHURCH STUDY COURSE began October 1, 1959. It is a merger of three courses previously promoted by the Sunday School Board —the Sunday School Training Course, the Graded Training Union Study Course, and the Church Music Training Course. On October 1, 1961, the Woman's Missionary Union principles and methods studies were added. On January 1, 1967, the Brotherhood Commission principles and methods studies were added.

The course is fully graded. The system of awards provides a series of five diplomas of twenty books each for Adults or Young People, two diplomas of five books each for Intermediates, and two diplomas of five books each for Juniors.

The course is comprehensive, with books grouped into twenty-one categories. The purpose of the course is to help Christians to grow in knowledge and conviction, to help them to grow toward maturity in Christian character and competence for service, to encourage them to participate worthily as workers in their churches, and to develop leaders for all phases of church life and work.

The Church Study Course is promoted by the Baptist Sunday School Board, 127 Ninth Avenue, North, Nashville, Tennessee 37203, through its Sunday School, Training Union, Church Music, and Church Administration Departments; by the Woman's Missionary Union, 600 North Twentieth Street, Birmingham, Alabama 35203; by the Brotherhood Commission, 1548 Poplar Avenue, Memphis, Tennessee 38104; and by the respective departments in the states affiliated with the Southern Baptist Convention. A description of the course and the system of awards may be found in the leaflet "Trained Workmen," which may be obtained without charge from any one of these departments.

A record of all awards earned should be maintained in each church. A person should be designated by the church to keep the files. Forms for such records may be ordered from any Baptist Book Store.

Requirements for Credit for Class or Home Study

If credit is desired for the study of this book in class or by the home study method, the following requirements must be met:

I. CLASS METHOD

1. The class must meet a minimum of six clock hours. The required time does not include assembly periods.
2. A class member who attends all class sessions and reads the book will not be required to do any written work.
3. A class member who is absent from one or more class sessions must read the book and answer the questions on all chapters he misses.
4. The teacher should request an award for himself. A person who teaches a book in sections for Intermediates or Juniors of any category or conducts an approved unit of instruction for Nursery, Beginner, or Primary children will be granted an award in category 11, Special Studies, which will count as an elective on his own diploma. He should specify in his request the name of the book taught, or unit conducted for Nursery, Beginner, or Primary children.

   Credit will be given to "team-teachers" when they co-operatively plan the teaching procedures and attend and share responsibility in each teaching session.
5. The teacher should complete the "Request for Book Award" (Form 151) and forward it to the Church Study Course Awards Office, 127 Ninth Avenue, North, Nashville, Tennessee 37203.

II. INDIVIDUAL HOME STUDY

1. A person who does not attend any class session may receive credit by answering all questions for written work as indicated in the book or in a designated periodical. When a person turns in his paper on home study, he must certify that he has read the book.
2. Students may find profit in studying the text together, but individual papers are required. Carbon copies or duplicates in any form cannot be accepted.

3. Home study work papers may be graded by the pastor or a person designated by him, or they may be sent to the Church Study Course Awards Office for grading. The form entitled "Request for Book Award" (Form 151) must be used in requesting awards. It should be mailed to the Church Study Course Awards Office, 127 Ninth Avenue, North, Nashville, Tennessee 37203.

4. Credit for home study of mission study books not containing questions is earned by writing a synopsis of each chapter.

III. CREDIT FOR THIS BOOK

This book is number 32 in category 2, section for Adults and Young People.

Acknowledgments

BELOW IS A LIST of those books most frequently consulted by the author in preparation of the manuscript for this book. The use of these books does not imply endorsement of the full contents of any of them.

Abba, R. "Priests and Levites," *The Interpreter's Dictionary of the Bible*. New York: Abingdon Press, 1962.

Bamberger, B. J. "Tax Collector," *The Interpreter's Dictionary of the Bible*.

Barth, Gerhard. "Matthew's Understanding of the Law," *Tradition and Interpretation in Matthew* by Gunther Bornkamm, Gerhard Barth, and Heinz Joachim Held. Philadelphia: Westminster Press, 1963.

Bowman, J. W. *The Intention of Jesus*. Philadelphia: Westminster Press, 1943.

Browning, W. R. F. *The Gospel According to Saint Luke*. New York: Collier Books, 1962.

Cadbury, J. J. *Beginnings of Christianity*, II, 489–501. New York: Harper & Row, 1952.

Confezmann, Hans. *The Theology of St. Luke*. New York: Harper & Row, 1960.

Creed, J. M. *The Gospel According to Saint Luke*. London: MacMillan, 1950.

Dana, H. E. *The New Testament World*. Nashville: Broadman Press, 1944.

Easton, Burton Scott. *The Gospel According to Saint Luke*. Edinburgh: T. & T. Clark, 1926.

Geldenhuys, Norval. *Commentary of the Gospel of Luke*. Grand Rapids: Eerdmans, 1952.

Gilmour, MacLean. *The Gospel According to Saint Luke*. New York: Abingdon-Cokesbury Press, 1952.

Gollwitzer, Helmut. *Die Freude Gottes, Einfuhrung in das Lukasevangelium*. Berlin-Dahlem: Burckhandthaus-Verlag, 1952.

Hebert, A. G. *The Throne of David*. London: Faber and Faber, 1941.

Leaney, A. R. C. *The Gospel According to Saint Luke*. New York: Harper & Row, 1952.

McDowell, E. A. *Jesus and His Cross*. Nashville: Broadman Press, 1944. (Formerly *Son of Man and Suffering Servant*.)

Manson, William. *The Gospel of Luke*. New York: Harper & Row, 1930.

Manson, William. *Jesus the Messiah*. Philadelphia: Westminster Press, 1946.

The New English Bible. Cambridge: Oxford University Press, 1961.

Plummer, Alfred. *The Gospel According to Saint Luke*. Edinburgh: T. & T. Clark, 1901.

Rengstorf, Karl Heinrich. "Das Neue Testament Deutsch," *Das Evangelium nach Lukas*. Gottingen: Vandenhoeck & Ruprecht, 1955.

Robertson, A. T. *A Harmony of the Gospels for Students of the Life of Christ*. New York: Harper & Row, 1922.

Rowley, H. H. "The Baptism of John and the Qumran Sect," *New Testament Essays*. Manchester: University Press, 1959.

Rowlington, D. T. "Synoptic Problem," *The Interpreter's Dictionary of the Bible*. (Vol. IV), New York: Abingdon Press, 1962.

Stagg, Frank. *The Book of Acts, the Early Struggle for an Unhindered Gospel*. Nashville: Broadman Press, 1955.

Stagg, Frank. *New Testament Theology*. Nashville: Broadman Press, 1962.

Tinsley, E. J. *The Gospel According to Luke*. Cambridge: University Press, 1965.

Part 1

INTRODUCING THE GOSPEL OF LUKE
Luke 1:1–4

AT THE HEART of Luke's Gospel is the picture of a shepherd rejoicing over the recovery of a lost sheep, a woman rejoicing over the recovery of a lost coin, and a father rejoicing over the recovery of one son and pleading with another son to join the family in joyous reunion (chap. 15). God is like that. In brief, that is what the Gospel of Luke is about. It is about God's concern for all people, his joy over each one recovered—Jew, Samaritan, or Gentile. It is about God's concern with all the needs of all people: that the blind see, the deaf hear, the lame walk, the lepers be cleansed, those in bondage be freed, and that sinners be forgiven. It is just such a Gospel which now we are privileged to study.

The Gospel of Luke will be studied in five parts. These parts represent natural divisions within Luke's Gospel, recognized by almost all scholars. These units are not of uniform length; but they are clearly distinguishable, and each serves a purpose in Luke's unfolding of the gospel. The five units are: (1) Luke's preface, discussed under the heading, Introducing the Gospel of Luke (1:1–4); (2) Preparation for the Ministry (1:5 to 4:13); (3) Ministry in Galilee (4:14 to 9:50); (4) Journeying Toward Jerusalem (9:51 to 19:27); and (5) Jesus' Ministry in Jerusalem (19:28 to 24:53).

The headings designating the five parts under which this study is organized seek not only to preserve the natural divisions of Luke's Gospel, but also to trace the external or geographical movement found in the Gospel.

1

The ten chapter headings have been chosen to bring out the depth of the movement within Luke's Gospel, developed under the theme, "The Gospel for All People." The Christ portrayed by Luke was concerned to minister to all people in terms of all their needs. Luke showed how these wider concerns of Jesus brought him into conflict with the institutional religion of his own people. Luke's Gospel shows that Christianity began with Jesus of Nazareth, within orthodox Judaism, and among Jewish people of true piety. When Luke wrote, Christianity had become a worldwide fellowship, no longer bound to Palestine, the Jewish nation, or the synagogues. Chapters 2–10, organized under parts two through five, will follow Luke's tracing of this amazing development.

Part one will be based on Luke's preface (1:1–4). In these four verses, Luke disclosed his purpose and message, his awareness of previous narratives about Jesus, and his method of research. In this part, inquiry will also be made into the setting or life situation out of which Luke's Gospel came and the relationship of Luke's Gospel to the book of Acts and to the other Gospels.

1

The Gospel for All People

1:1-4

HAPPILY FOR US, Luke wrote a preface to his Gospel as well as to the book of Acts. Much valuable information is thus given about Luke's purpose and message, the relationship of his work to that of others, and his method of research. From the whole of Luke's two volumes, the Gospel and Acts, we may conclude much about the life situation out of which Luke wrote and the bearing of this upon his purpose and message.

I. AUTHORSHIP AND DATE

Early tradition ascribed the Third Gospel and Acts to Luke, the "beloved physician" (Col. 4:14) and companion to Paul (2 Tim. 4:11). Luke is not otherwise prominent, and there are no substantial reasons for doubting the tradition that he wrote the Third Gospel and Acts. This is not to overlook the fact that the four Gospels and Acts are anonymous. Unlike Paul, the writer did not affix his name to his work.

Luke's two volumes probably were written after A.D. 70, not necessarily long afterwards. It was in A.D. 70 that Jerusalem and the Temple were destroyed by the Romans. The Jewish-Roman War of A.D. 66–70 probably provided the occasion for the final break between synagogue and church or Judaism and Christianity. Luke-Acts seems to reflect this stage of development. If Luke used Mark, as is generally recognized, this bears upon the dating of Luke.[1] Mark probably was written around A.D. 65, because it seems to reflect the crisis situation brought on by the persecution of Christians under the Emperor Nero, who unjustly blamed them for burning Rome in A.D. 64.

II. PURPOSE AND MESSAGE

Luke began with a long, carefully balanced sentence, commonly called his preface:

Since indeed many have undertaken to draw up a narrative concerning the matters having been brought to fulfilment among us, just as those who were from the beginning eyewitnesses and servants of the word delivered unto us, it seemed good to me also, having traced accurately, and in order, all things from the beginning, to write to you, excellent Theophilus, so that you might know the certainty concerning the things which you were taught (1:1-4).[2]

The purpose which Luke had in common with other Gospel writers was to portray Jesus Christ and the salvation which he offers. Each Gospel was written to tell the story of Christ in such a way as to bring people to faith in him and to nurture those who believe. The writers of the Gospels used sources, written and oral, but they were not mere compilers or ordinary chroniclers. Each was an author concerned about interpreting the words and deeds which he recorded. And he related them to his own generation and life situation, as he was guided by the Holy Spirit. Each Gospel is to be studied as a whole, a literary unit with a theological purpose. While all the Gospels have a common purpose, there is the

---

[1] See A. T. Robertson, *A Harmony of the Gospels for Students of the Life of Christ* (New York: Harper & Bros., 1922), v. ii, where Robertson traces back to 1892 his proposal to John A. Broadus that he construct a "harmony" based upon the assumption of the priority of Mark and its use by Matthew and Luke.

[2] Unless otherwise indicated, translations from the Greek New Testament will be the author's.

purpose that is peculiar to each. Let us look now at Luke's distinctive purpose.

1. *To Give Certainty*

Luke addressed his two volumes to "Theophilus," his concern being made explicit in the words " . . . that you might know the certainty concerning the things in which you were instructed" (Luke 1:4). (The Greek name Theophilus means "friend of God." Whether Luke had in mind a particular individual or a typical "friend of God" cannot be determined.) Luke had made careful study of the written and oral witnesses (Luke 1:1-3) to what Jesus had done and taught (Acts 1:1); and he had set himself to the task of drawing up an orderly and accurate narrative of what had been accomplished among them (1:1).

It is clear that Luke was first of all dealing with something that actually took place in history. Luke's word for "certainty" (1:4) may be used to mean "the actual truth." Moffatt translated the Greek word "solid truth." Christianity is bound up with an event in history. It is not a speculative system which began as an inquiry into, or search for, philosophical, theological, or ethical truths or values. All four Gospels are concerned with the theological meaning of certain events in history, but they are anything but disinterested in history. For them history does matter.

Early Christians trusted and worshiped a risen Lord, but never did their interest lag with respect to "the historical Jesus." Many "narratives" had been drawn up concerning him; and from the first, "eyewitnesses" had related what they had seen. It is inconceivable that those who saw and heard Jesus would not, during his lifetime, repeat many of his sayings and describe to one another things which he did. Jesus was not the kind of person who could be ignored or forgotten. How could they forget or be silent about one who so upset his home synagogue that they tried to push him off a cliff, who set aside cherished sabbath customs, and who ate with "publicans and sinners" (society's outcasts)? Besides, Jesus called certain ones to be with him, and he taught them things which they were to pass on to others. As new followers came into the Christian community, they were "instructed" in these things which occurred. These were "matters" which could be "traced out," verified or proven.

How did Christianity get started? Luke said that it began with something done, something accomplished. It began with an event in history. It was bound up with persons as real as Zacharias and Elizabeth, Joseph and Mary, Simeon and Anna. It was bound up with places as specific and concrete as Bethlehem, Nazareth, and Jerusalem. What Luke wrote about was concerned with a real person in real history. It concerned flesh and blood, tears and laughter, eating and drinking, living and dying, work and play, storms and stillness, cities and countrysides, hope and fear, love and hate, trust and betrayal.

Luke wrote, not about something that merely happened, but something that was *accomplished* by studied purpose (1:1). He wrote history, but not just history. He wrote salvation-history—something which God was doing in the world, supremely in Jesus of Nazareth. What he wrote was not history working itself out, but God working in history; it was not an accident in history, but the fulfilment of long and incessant hopes through a mighty act of God.

2. *To Present an Orderly Account*

By "in order," Luke did not mean that he was primarily concerned to put all the events in chronological order. In the main, this may follow; but he did not bind himself to such a purpose. For example, in 4:16–30, Luke featured an incident in the synagogue at Nazareth. As references in the story itself reflect, there had been previous work in Capernaum; but Luke deliberately passed over these earlier works in order to feature the Nazareth incident. No doubt the reason for this was that the Nazareth experience was best suited to Luke's purpose of showing the nature of Jesus' ministry and its reception. By "in order," Luke seems to refer to the logical arrangement of his material in such a way as to develop his theme—the gospel for all people.

3. To Trace the Emergence of a Worldwide Fellowship

Luke's special purpose may best be seen when his two volumes, the Gospel and Acts, are considered together. The two volumes trace the Christian movement from its beginnings with Jesus of Nazareth to its development into a worldwide fellowship transcending the limits of Jewish nationality and giving place impartially to Jews, Samaritans, and Gentiles. For Luke, Jesus was "no mere Jewish Messiah, but a World-Saviour, the founder of a world-religion" (Manson).

Luke was concerned about the fears, prejudices, separations, hostilities, and even violence which marked relationships between Jews and Christians. He was aware of the tension between champions of Jewish exclusiveness and those who saw that in Christ the walls of separation must fall. Positively, Luke traced a history, or development, which began within Judaism and became a universal movement, rising above worldly distinctions such as nationality, race, and status.

III. THE LIFE SITUATION

1. Early Spread into Larger World

When Luke wrote his two volumes, Christianity had already established itself in the larger world; and it was becoming increasingly a Gentile fellowship. Luke's task was not so much to urge that Christ be preached to the Gentiles, for that was being done, as it was to justify that fact and support this mission. In his two volumes, Luke traced the history of Christianity from a movement within Judaism to a worldwide fellowship. Crossing geographical boundaries had been easy. Within a few years, Christianity had spread far and wide: northward at least as far as Damascus and Syrian Antioch; southward into Egypt and Ethiopia; westward to Cyprus, Cyrene, the Aegean basin, and Rome. An eastern extension of Christianity toward Babylon may be assumed, but Luke does not trace it. From chapter two of Acts, it is learned that Jews from all over the Greco-Roman world, from Mesopotamia to Rome, were in Jerusalem on that day of Pentecost when the Holy Spirit came in such power. There were Jewish synagogues all over the Greco-Roman world, and Christianity rapidly spread through these channels.

2. Lines Most Difficult to Cross

The boundaries most difficult to cross were not geographical; they were those artificial distinctions which separated Jews, Samaritans, and Gentiles from one another. These distinctions had to be broken down. Luke's Gospel shows that Jesus began this process by rejecting the superficial distinction which the Pharisees had made between "the righteous" and "the sinners." Jesus found all to be sinners and all to be in need of the same salvation. With equal freedom, he offered himself to Pharisees and publicans (tax-gatherers, considered by the Pharisees as unclean). In the book of Acts, Luke showed how what Jesus had begun—making no distinction between Pharisees and publicans—was extended to all people. He told how the gospel was preached to Jews, Samaritans, Gentiles who were attracted to Judaism and were under the instruction of the synagogue, and even to persons who had not been under the influence of the synagogue.

When Luke wrote, the Christian community in outward appearance was quite unlike what may have been expected of it by those who saw its beginnings. It began in Palestine;

now it was found all over the Mediterranean world. Jesus and all his early followers were Jews. Now the church was predominantly non-Jewish. Jesus and his earliest followers went by custom to the synagogues and the Temple. At the time of Luke's writing, many Christians were meeting in homes and public buildings. The Temple had been destroyed, and the synagogue doors were closing or had been closed to Christians.

3. Christianity True to Its Origins

Was Christianity untrue to Judaism? Was it untrue to its beginnings? Luke will answer that it was indeed true to Judaism at its best and to its own beginnings. Christianity was born within truest Judaism. It did not forsake synagogues or Temple. Christians were gradually *excluded* from the synagogues and Temple because Christianity *included* any who by faith would become a follower of Jesus Christ. The earliest and bitterest hostility to Jesus was not because he claimed to be the Christ, but because he "received sinners." He was criticized because he mingled freely with people who did not comply with Pharisaic requirements about the sabbath, food laws, purification rites, fasting, and the like.

In the Gospel and Acts, we see the true concern of Jesus for all people, not Jews alone. He was concerned for all the needs of all people. Jesus was not concerned for the institutions of religion as such: sabbath, fasting, purification rites, and so on. His concern was for God and for people. He spelled out his sense of mission both in an early sermon in the synagogue at Nazareth (4:14–30) and in his reply to the messengers of the imprisoned John the Baptist (7:19–23). The crucifixion of Jesus resulted from this basic conflict between Jesus and institutional religion, both Pharisaic and Sadducean. Jesus did not leave the synagogue or Temple because he wanted to leave. He was thrown out of the synagogue in Nazareth (4:29), and he was rejected in Jerusalem

(19:41–48; 23:1–2). The Christian community of Luke's day had not broken faith with true Judaism nor with Jesus Christ. In becoming a fellowship of persons above the distinctions of nationality, race, and ritual, Christianity is true to Judaism and to Christ.

IV. RELATIONSHIP TO THE BOOK OF ACTS

The preface to Luke's Gospel (1:1–4) and the preface to Acts (1:1–5) tie the two books together. Not only are both books by the same author; the two books develop one continuing theme. Both are concerned with what God accomplished in Jesus Christ. The first "treatise" was concerned with "all that Jesus began both to do and to teach until he was received up" (Acts 1:1–2). The second book shows what the risen Christ continued to do through the Holy Spirit and through the church.

In the Gospel of Luke, Christ is shown to be offering himself in a ministry to persons of all kinds and in all their needs. His bitterest opponents were the Pharisees who were concerned with the institutional aspects of religion and the Sadducees who were concerned with maintaining the status quo. (As collaborators with their Roman conquerors, the Sadducees held powerful and lucrative positions in the Temple.) Jesus put man above the sabbath (6:5,9). He made no real distinction between harlots and publicans on the one hand and self-righteous religionists on the other. All were placed under the same judgment and offered the same salvation. Because of this, he was rejected and crucified.

In Acts, Luke developed this same theme.[3] In the early chapters, we see Jewish Christianity reaching thousands in Jerusalem. The real conflict began when Stephen and others preached that God was never limited to one land or temple.

---

[3] For a study of Luke's purpose in Acts, see Frank Stagg, *The Book of Acts, the Early Struggle for an Unhindered Gospel* (Nashville: Broadman Press, 1955).

In Acts, Luke traced out the long struggle for an unhindered gospel. A great victory was won by the inclusion of all who would come into this fellowship. A consequent tragedy was the self-exclusion of many Jews who were unwilling to be a part of a fellowship which made no distinction between Jew and non-Jew.

V. RELATIONSHIP TO OTHER GOSPELS

Most scholars believe that one of the narratives which Luke (1:1–4) alluded to was the Gospel of Mark. They believe that he used Mark as one of his basic sources. Matthew likewise is thought to have used Mark as one of his sources. All but about sixty verses of Mark have parallels in Luke or Matthew, or both. Luke used about one-half of Mark and Matthew almost all of it.

All four Gospels have the same basic purpose: to present Jesus as Christ the Saviour and Lord. But each Gospel has its own special interest. Since his Gospel was probably written as Christians were being persecuted by Emperor Nero, Mark wrote to assure Christians that Jesus, the Son of God, had been completely triumphant, though seemingly weak and humble. Through his death and resurrection, the Suffering Servant showed himself to be the triumphant Son of God.

Matthew cannot be reduced to a simple analysis. He wrote some time after Mark, fighting on at least two fronts. From without were the Pharisaic charges that Christianity was morally lax and that salvation could come only through keeping the Jewish law. From within was the threat of moral and ethical failure, for some twisted grace and freedom into license. Matthew showed that true Israel survives in Christ, that in Christ the covenants with Abraham and David are fulfilled, and that in Christ are both God's gift of grace and his moral demand. Salvation is God's work, and it is good work. The righteousness which God requires is greater than that of the scribes and Pharisees. It is inner and not just outward righteousness. But this righteousness is God's achievement in those who by faith will receive it; it is not man's achievement, as the Pharisees would hold.

John wrote last of all and for a situation which had developed beyond that known when the Synoptic Gospels (Mark, Luke, and Matthew) were written. He wrote when threats came from many sides. There were Jews who were claiming for the law what John claimed for Christ. There were followers of John the Baptist who needed to be reminded that John's true hearers followed Jesus. There were Gnostics or Gnostic-like people who held to the deity of Christ but explained away his humanity. John's task was to restate the gospel in language which would be understandable to a new age and which would meet the needs on many fronts.

Luke wrote some time after Mark, possibly in Syrian Antioch. He presented Jesus as the Saviour who meets every human need, one who offers salvation to all who will receive it. Luke demonstrated how Jesus gave special attention to those who were normally overlooked or discriminated against: the poor people, children, women, Samaritans, the "publicans and sinners."

Luke also pointed up Jesus' warning against Mammon, the god of money or things. Jesus purposed to free man of all tyranny, including that of the material. It is to be observed that Jesus kept two things in balance: the concern that the physical and material needs of people be met, and the concern that things not be served as though they were gods. Just as he had placed personal values over material ones, Jesus offered true religion over against both institutional religion and secularism or materialism.

VI. LUKE'S METHOD

In his preface (1:1-4), Luke set forth something of his method in research and writing. He had carefully traced out the story of the deeds and words of Jesus. He had knowledge of earlier narratives which had been developed under the control of "eyewitnesses and ministers of the word." Luke used a Greek term for "tradition" (1:2), just as did Paul (2 Thess. 2:15). By this he referred to what had been transmitted concerning the words and deeds of Jesus. This "tradition" began to take shape from the earliest days. Those who heard and saw Jesus did what is natural. They talked among themselves about these things, and they told other people about what they had heard and seen.

Possibly the early Christians gathered in homes or courtyards night after night, building their fellowship and services around a meal. It would be normal for those who had seen and heard Jesus to tell about it. "I remember," or "Do you remember?" would be oft repeated words. Those who had not seen or heard Jesus would naturally ask about him. Then, too, as needs would arise in the community, Christians would turn to what Jesus had done and said to find answers for problems. In this way the community remembered Jesus, formulated narratives about him, and made collections of his sayings.

The "tradition" thus grew and was transmitted, at first orally and then in written form. Luke gave careful attention to these narratives, and seemingly used some of them as his sources. He did not actually say that he talked with eyewitnesses. But he did write that those who delivered the traditions from the beginning were eyewitnesses. Probably Luke did consult eyewitnesses as well as written sources. Paul attested to the fact that upwards of five hundred persons to whom the risen Christ had appeared were alive when he wrote to the Corinthians (1 Cor. 15:6). Luke may well have known many of these eyewitnesses during Paul's lifetime, and some of them may have been alive when Luke wrote.

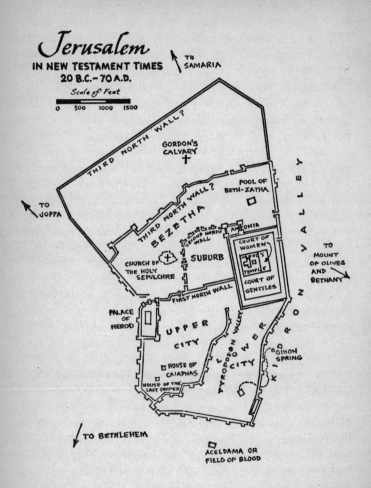

Jerusalem
IN NEW TESTAMENT TIMES
20 B.C. – 70 A.D.

Scale of Feet

0   500   1000   1500

TO SAMARIA

THIRD NORTH WALL ?

GORDON'S CALVARY

TO JOPPA

THIRD NORTH WALL ?

POOL OF BETH-ZATHA

BEZETHA

SECOND NORTH WALL

ANTONIA

CHURCH OF THE HOLY SEPULCHRE

SUBURB

COURT OF WOMEN

HEROD'S TEMPLE

COURT OF GENTILES

TO MOUNT OF OLIVES AND BETHANY

FIRST NORTH WALL

PALACE OF HEROD

UPPER CITY

TYROPOEON VALLEY

LOWER CITY

KIDRON VALLEY

GIHON SPRING

HOUSE OF CAIAPHAS

HOUSE OF THE LAST SUPPER

TO BETHLEHEM

ACELDAMA OR FIELD OF BLOOD

Part 2

PREPARATION FOR THE MINISTRY

Luke 1:5 to 4:13

PART TWO WILL CONSIST of two chapters: "Jesus' Early Years" (1:5 to 2:52) and "Special Preparation for Public Ministry" (3:1 to 4:13). This division of Luke's Gospel is concerned with the births of John the Baptist and Jesus, the infancy and childhood of Jesus, the preaching of John, and the response of Jesus. All of this appears on the surface of Luke's narrative, obvious even to the casual reader. But a study in depth of Part Two should disclose something more of Luke's special purpose. This portion of Luke's Gospel points up the Jewish origins of a movement soon to become prevailingly Gentile.

At the time of Luke's writing, the Christian movement was becoming predominantly Gentile. Probably Christianity and Judaism were being seen as unrelated religions. Church and synagogue were going separate ways. Christians would gather in homes, courtyards, and rented buildings rather than in the synagogues. This practice naturally brought questions about the relationship between Judaism and the Christian community. Was Christianity a false religion? Was it untrue to Old Testament Judaism? Was the Christian movement born outside true Judaism?

In Part Two may be seen the thoroughly Jewish origins of John and Jesus. Both were born into homes of genuine piety. They were nurtured from the Scriptures in homes loyal to synagogue and Temple. Zacharias, Elizabeth, Joseph,

15

Mary, Simeon, and Anna represented Jewish faith and piety at its best. John was from a priestly family. Jesus grew up in a home of such piety that the family made yearly pilgrimages to the Temple in Jerusalem (2:22–39,41,42). Jesus knew the Temple as his Father's house (2:49). Thus, Christian origins were within the faith of Israel.

Jesus did not bypass his own people. By the time of Luke's writing, the Christian community was Gentile. It had gone outside the framework of institutional Judaism, but Jesus had begun his work with the Jews. This section will set the stage for Part Three, in which it will be seen that Jesus did not leave the synagogue; he was thrown out. Jesus did not reject his people; they rejected him. The church did not leave the synagogue; it was excluded. The truest Judaism, according to Luke-Acts, survived in the movement which had its origin and impulse in Jesus of Nazareth.

2

Jesus' Early Years

1:5 to 2:52

EXCEPT FOR THE PREFACE (1:1–4), chapters two and three of Luke's Gospel are devoted to the birth and childhood of Jesus. John the Baptist, too, is prominent in the story; but he is given this place in the story only because of his relationship with Jesus. These two chapters in Luke show God's initiative behind the ministries of John and Jesus. They show the sense of God's presence felt by those who surround John and Jesus in their early years. Awe, worship, and gratitude strongly mark these two chapters.

I. ANNOUNCEMENTS AND A VISIT (1:5–56)

1. Concerning the Birth of John (1:5–25)

Zacharias and Elizabeth were both of priestly families. Luke wrote that she was a descendant of Aaron and he a priest of the course of Abijah (1:5). Since Abijah was a descendant of Aaron (1 Chron. 24:10), Zacharias, too, was of the line of Aaron. There were so many priests that they had been divided into twenty-four courses or groups (1 Chron. 24:1,4), each group serving in rotation for a week at a time, beginning with the sabbath, except at the great annual festivals when all of the priests officiated together. While the number of lower priests was large, there was a very small number of high priests. They came from a few wealthy families which were associated with the Sadducean party. At

17

that time, the Sadducees collaborated with the Romans, conquerors and rulers of the Jews since about 63 B.C. Many of the lower priests were of truer piety than was to be found among the high priests.

The lower priests are also to be distinguished from the Pharisees, who were "laymen." Although the Pharisees had much to do with the way Temple services were observed, the actual performance of the rituals at the Temple was in the hands of the priests. The Pharisees exercised their chief function through the synagogues and gradually took over much of the teaching function which formerly belonged to the priests. From among the Sadducees, came the high priests who presided over the Sanhedrin, the highest court of the Jews. Through collaboration with the Romans, the Sadducees largely controlled the Temple.

Zacharias probably belonged to the group of about 20,000 lower priests who, in their rotating twenty-four courses, performed the daily and seasonal rituals at the Temple.

Zacharias and Elizabeth were devout, upright, and obedient servants of God. They stood in striking contrast to the wicked Herod the Great, king of the Jews (40–4 B.C.), reflecting a true piety in those dark days of Herod. Their great sorrow was that they were without children, and their advanced years seemed to deny them hope of having any.

A once-in-a-lifetime privilege came to Zacharias when the lot fell upon him to offer the incense in the Temple. There were three hours of prayer each day, incense being offered at the first and third of these hours, early morning and about the middle of the afternoon. (See Ex. 30:7–8; Psalm 141:2.)

As Zacharias was at the altar of incense, an angel appeared on the right side of the altar. Uncertain of its implication, Zacharias was greatly troubled by this appearance. The angel comforted him with the assurance that his supplication was heard and that his wife Elizabeth would bear him a son, to be called John. Whether or not significance is to be seen in their Hebrew names, Zacharias means "God remembered"; Elizabeth means "God's oath"; and John means "God is gracious." John's birth would bring joy and gladness to many people. Joy is a dominant note in Luke's Gospel.

John's work would be "to make ready for the Lord a people who had been prepared" (1:17). Through many centuries, God had been preparing Israel for the salvation which in its fulness was to come in Jesus Christ. John's work was to get these people ready for the actual appearance of their promised Christ. Empowered by the Holy Spirit, he would accomplish this by turning the children of Israel to their God and to one another. This was to be a dual reconciliation: man reconciled to God and, thus, man reconciled to man. The New Testament knows no reconciliation to God which does not change man's attitude toward his fellowman.

A second mark of John's work of reconciliation was to be righteousness. The "disobedient" were to be turned to "the wisdom of the righteous." The mention of fathers and children in verse 17 may refer to the turning of the disobedient sons of John's generation to the patriarchal faith. However, it probably refers to something nearer at hand, actual family relationships where basic morality and religion must begin.

Zacharias, for all his piety, suffered a rebuke as a result of his lack of faith. He doubted the promise of a son because of his advanced age and that of his wife (1:18). Luke's Gospel is the story of God's coming to man with the gift of salvation dependent upon the demand of faith and obedience. Zacharias remained speechless until after the birth of John, because he had not trusted God's promise.

2. Concerning the Birth of Jesus (1:26–38)

This is a most important section. Here is the angel's announcement to the virgin Mary. Here is the promise of the gift of a son who would occupy "the throne of David" and whose kingdom (reign) would be forever.

Luke proclaimed the <u>miraculous conception</u> of Jesus, as did Matthew (1:18–25). The term "miraculous conception" is to be preferred to "virgin birth," because it places the emphasis where Luke and Matthew place it—upon God's act rather than Mary's state. The fact that both Luke and Matthew knew this story and apparently wrote independently of one another indicates that the story is older than either Gospel. The point of the story of Jesus' miraculous conception is to show how fully his coming into the world as Saviour and his establishment of an eternal kingdom is of God and not of man. It shows how helpless man was to bring about his own salvation or to bring about the kingdom of God—as helpless as were Elizabeth in her old age and Mary as a virgin to produce children of themselves. The story shows how utterly dependent man is upon God for salvation, even as Zacharias had to learn to trust God's word (1:20) and Mary had to learn that with God there is no impossibility (1:37). It shows how freely God gives in all that he does.

Jesus was both virgin born and sinless, but Luke did not tell of the virgin birth in order to account for Jesus' sinlessness. The deity and sinlessness of Jesus do not depend upon the virtue or virginity of Mary. He is Son of God, not because of Mary, but because of the Holy Spirit. Jesus was conceived of the Holy Spirit and, hence, is "Son of God" (1:35). He was tempted yet did not sin, and in his own right he is sinless and righteous (4:1–13). Mary was not sinless, and Luke did not say that sin is inherited from the male parent rather than the mother. Mary was not the fountain of grace; she was the recipient of grace (1:28,30). The victory over sin was not accomplished in Mary; it was accomplished in Jesus Christ alone.

The miraculous conception of Jesus is the gospel of grace. It is the story of God's initiative and God's mighty act of salvation. When Mary was promised a son, she did not see how this could be (1:29). A virgin of herself cannot bear a son.

This is the point. Mary could not bear a son, but God could give her one: "For nothing shall be impossible with God" (1:37). Man cannot produce his own salvation, but God can give him salvation. Like Zacharias and Mary, man must trust God and receive God's gift.

The kingdom of God and the salvation of man were announced in a most amazing way—in terms of a tiny babe! Incredible, yet it is to be believed. This the Gospel proclaims, and each person can only accept or reject it. He cannot change it.

3. Concerning Mary's Visits to Elizabeth (1:39-56)

The stories of John and Jesus are brought together in the meeting of their mothers. Mary was hailed as "blessed among women." This verse has been misapplied with respect to Mary. She was hailed as the object or recipient of grace, not as the source or fountain of grace. In verse 43, Elizabeth addressed Mary as "mother of my Lord [kyrios]," not as "mother of God [theos]." The deity of Christ is not in question, but Mary is not the mother of God. God has no mother. Mary was the mother of Jesus of Nazareth, the truly human one in whom God was incarnate. This is not quibbling about fine points of language. It is to avoid giving to Mary a place not assigned to her by the New Testament. Jesus Christ is Son of God and son of Mary, but Mary is not God's mother.

The Magnificat derives its name from the first word of the Latin version of 1:46-55. This beautifully poetic passage is in praise of God, proclaiming his greatness as expressed in mercy to the lowly. In early Old Latin manuscripts and in manuscripts known to early scholars such as Irenaeus, Origen, and Jerome, verse 46 reads: "And Elizabeth said ...." All Greek manuscripts attribute the Magnificat to Mary; and this is probably correct, although the evidence is not decisive.

The Magnificat is modeled upon the Song of Hannah (1

Sam. 2:1–10). This early Christian psalm is in praise of God.
It is marked by joy and gratitude. God is praised for his
mighty acts. Mercy is seen to be the divine impulse behind
both judgment and redemption, behind the overthrowing
of the haughty, and the upbuilding of the lowly. It is an
act of mercy to free the proud from vain self-trust, even as
it is mercy which feeds the hungry and lifts the downtrod-
den.

II. PROPHECY FULFILLED (1:57 to 2:20)

1. *In the Birth of John* (1:57–80)

Again Luke depicted the beginnings of Christianity in
Judaism at its best. Awe, worship, and gratitude are marks
of many pious Jews who recognized in John the Baptist and
in Jesus God's world of light and peace breaking into man's
world of darkness and strife. The phrase which Zacharias
used, "dayspring from on high" (1:78), are words used to
mean messianic redemption, or the Messiah himself. Literally,
the words mean "the dawn" or "the rising sun." The words
of Zacharias described not an upward surge of humanity,
struggling toward a better world, but rather the gospel of
a divine visitation. God has come to man to redeem his people
(1:68). This salvation is an act of deliverance; God is keeping his covenant (1:72f). It is an act of mercy (1:72a);
it is a gift to sinners (1:77). At the same time, this salvation
is demanding. Sinners are forgiven and delivered from their
sins that they might serve God in holiness and righteousness
(1:77). God gives himself and his salvation to sinners who
submit to his kingship as ultimate and absolute.

2. *In the Birth of Jesus* (2:1–20)

In many respects, Luke's stories of John and Jesus are
parallel, but at this point the superiority of Jesus over John
is shown. John's birth was an occasion for great joy, but he

was not worshiped. Jesus was acclaimed "Saviour, who is Christ the Lord" (2:11).

Luke's concern for a gospel for all people is reflected in the fact that he put the story of Jesus' birth in a world setting. Although Jesus was born into a thoroughly Jewish home, he was also born into the larger world which he came to save. Jesus was born under the Roman as well as under the Jewish law. Caesar Augustus, emperor of the Roman Empire, and Quirinius, governor of Syria, are mentioned along with Joseph and Mary, Bethlehem and Nazareth.

Difficult problems confront the scholar as he seeks to understand Luke's reference to "the first enrolment made when Quirinius was governor of Syria." Josephus (*Ant.* xviii. 2. 1) seems to place Quirinius and the census at least ten years too late to coincide with the birth of Jesus. Josephus reported that Quirinius carried out a census of Judea in A.D. 6. Jesus was born before Herod's death in 4 B.C.[1] The census in Luke, then, would need to be one that was otherwise unknown before Herod's death. Some find solution to the problem in that Quirinius was engaged in military operations on the northern frontiers of Cilicia between 10 B.C. and 7 B.C. These scholars consider it possible that Herod, under pressure of Quirinius, may have conducted a census to please the Romans. The birth of Jesus may have been a little later than 7 B.C. Allowing Jewish families to enrol according to ancient tribal identities would offset some of the offense at being compelled to engage in a Roman census.[2]

At Bethlehem Mary gave birth to a son, her firstborn (2:7). Had Luke wished to teach that Mary had no other children following her firstborn (*prōtotokos*), he could have

---

[1] Our calendar was developed in the sixth century by Dionysius Exiguus of Rome, and it is off by at least four years, due to his miscalculations as he replaced the Roman calendar with the Christian calendar.

[2] See Manson, *The Gospel of Luke,* pp. 16–17, for a discussion of this difficult problem.

used the word "only" (*monogenēs*). That Mary did have other children is explicit in 8:19-20 and in Mark 3:31-35.

The circumstances of the birth of Jesus defy all that the world would have expected of the coming of a Saviour. God came in a baby! The King of kings was born in the humblest of circumstances and was cradled in a manger. The birth of the Saviour was at first noticed only by humble people, like the shepherds, and by heaven.

Shepherds at Bethlehem were among the first to hear the news of a great joy intended for all people (2:10). Born in the City of David was a Saviour, Christ the Lord. Luke wrote his Gospel so as to show the Saviour's concern to save all people and to save each person in terms of his whole being.

Manuscripts differ in their reading of 2:14. Some have "good will toward men" while others have "peace . . . among men of good will." The reading best supported is as follows: "Glory to God in the highest; and upon earth, peace among men of [God's] good will." The birth of Jesus meant glory to God, for God's glorious character as redeemer would shine through this newborn one. The birth of Jesus also was conclusive evidence that man is the object of God's good will. God is for us (Rom. 8:31), not against us and not indifferent to us. Jesus Christ is God not only acting and speaking, but God uniquely present in a human life, having come to make himself known and to save mankind. The birth of Jesus was God's offer of peace to men, peace with God and with one another. In Jesus, peace has come for men who are the objects of God's good will.

The shepherds were the first to receive the announcement of the Saviour's birth and the first to visit the newborn babe. These simple people were representative of those called "the people of the land." They were not the learned scholars of the law nor those who prided themselves in the keeping of the law. They were the common people, overlooked or even despised by those who thought their study and observance of law earned them the right to salvation. But the gospel is not the story of reward for human achievement. It is the story of God's coming in mercy and grace to supply man's lack. Jesus came not to reward the righteous but to save sinners. (See 15:7,10,32.)

III. INFANCY AND CHILDHOOD OF JESUS (2:21–52)

1. *Circumcised and Presented* (2:21–40)

Major interest here is on the naming of Jesus, although the circumcision is also significant. The name Jesus (Greek) is the same as Joshua (Hebrew) and means Jehovah saves. The Gospel of Luke is largely the unfolding of what is implied in this name. Jesus Christ is God come to save sinners.

Jesus was circumcised on the eighth day after his birth, and Mary observed the purification rites in keeping with the Mosaic law. She went to Jerusalem to offer a sacrifice. (See Lev. 12.) Once again we are reminded by Luke that Jesus was born under the Jewish law and that Christianity is the fulfilment of Judaism. The offering of a pair of turtle doves and two young pigeons (2:24) indicates that Joseph and Mary were poor. The offering called for a lamb, but mothers who could not afford a lamb were permitted to substitute the less costly offering (Lev. 12:8).

Simeon seems to have been an old man, although this is not explicit. The long awaited promise that he would see "the consolation of Israel" was fulfilled when Simeon saw Jesus. He recognized Jesus as "the Lord's Christ" (2:26). Christ (the Greek equivalent of the Hebrew Messiah) means anointed, anointed to reign. Jesus is God's Christ, the one whom God anointed to reign. The kingdom of God is the sovereign rule of God, and it comes in the person of Jesus Christ. The name Jesus declares that Jehovah saves. The term Christ declares that God reigns in and through Jesus. He is Saviour and Lord. He is the Lord Christ, and before him every knee must ultimately bow (Phil. 2:10). Even the lost must finally answer to him as Lord. He is the sovereign Lord; he becomes one's Saviour when one submits to him in trust. One cannot know Jesus as Saviour only; he is Lord and Saviour. The lordship of Christ must be acknowledged by those who would follow him.

Having seen Jesus as God's promised salvation, Simeon was ready for release from his long task, death being the instrument of release (Plummer). It is made emphatic that salvation is offered "all peoples." This is a major theme in Luke-Acts. Much of what Luke wrote is the unfolding story of salvation offered to Jews and Gentiles alike, salvation which was widely received among the Jews first and then extended to the Gentiles. The admission of Gentiles into the Christian community became, however, a major problem. Many Jews were unwilling to receive uncircumcised Gentiles into the church fellowship, especially in view of the fact that table fellowship was at the center of early Christian life. (See Acts 10:15,28,34; 11:1–3,18; 21:20,27–31; 22:21; 26: 23; 28:25–28; Gal. 2:11–14.)

That Jesus would be rejected as well as accepted was anticipated in the words of Simeon (2:34). The fates of all would be determined in their encounter with him—one's reception of Christ determines his "rising" or his "falling." Even for Mary there would be "a sword" which would pierce her heart. Mary knew that her son was destined for a special work, but she understood little of its nature or means until after the death and resurrection of Jesus. Mary would lose her son before she gained him (8:19–21).

Anna was a devout Jewess prophetess, having spent most of her life at the Temple. It is not clear whether she was eighty-four years of age or that she had been a widow for eighty-four years. She is further evidence of the Jewish piety which surrounded Jesus and which formed the background to Christianity.

2. Visit to the Temple (2:41–52)

Again Jesus and his family are characterized as devout Jews. The family went every year to Jerusalem for the Passover celebration. The law required that every male go to Jerusalem for the Feasts of Passover, Pentecost, and Tabernacles (Ex. 23:14–17; 34:23; Deut. 16:16). Because of the wide dispersion of the Jews over the world from the time of the Exile, this law could not be observed strictly. Most Palestinian Jews tried to attend one feast each year. Women were not required to attend; but, out of piety, women like Mary did go to the feasts. The Passover celebrated God's deliverance of Israel from Egyptian bondage, and it was a rekindling of hopes that he would again send a Deliverer to Israel. Not only the immediate family of Jesus, but also their kinsfolk and friends were among those whose devotion took them to Jerusalem to worship.

Jesus became so absorbed at the Temple that he stayed. The family of Jesus was evidently preoccupied and left him behind as they began the homeward journey. Three days later Jesus was found in the Temple, talking with the doctors (teachers) of the Mosaic law. Jesus is not here presented as a "wonder boy," as he was in some of the apocryphal gospels of the second century; but he did amaze the teachers by his questions and answers. At twelve he was ready to assume the responsibilities of the law. He was a genuine learner.

Whereas the teachers were amazed at Jesus' answers, Joseph and Mary were astonished that their son had thus treated them (2:48). Jesus was respectful of parental authority, yet he recognized a higher claim—that of God as his true Father. Luke, having proclaimed the virgin birth of Jesus, did not hesitate to refer to Joseph and Mary as Jesus' parents or to Joseph as his father (2:41,48). Joseph was his legal father. But the point of verse 49 is not to be missed. To

Mary's claim, "thy father and I sought you in sorrow," Jesus replied, "Did you not know that I must be in my Father's house?" To deny that Jesus pondered his own identity and what was to be his work would be to make him less than man. At the age of twelve, he had an awareness of his relationship with God as his Father. This seems to have been the starting point or core to his growing understanding of his identity and role or work. By the time of his baptism, Jesus saw himself not only as God's Son; but also as one who was to accomplish his work in terms of the Suffering Servant depicted in Isaiah (Luke 3:23).

Luke affirmed that Jesus grew (2:40,52). Both the divinity and humanity of Jesus are taken seriously in Luke's Gospel. There were no "Docetics" (those who said that Christ only *seemed* to have a body) among those who knew Jesus in the days of his flesh. At a later time, the Docetics affirmed the deity but denied the humanity of Jesus. Luke affirmed both. Jesus was begotten of the Holy Spirit (1:35), and he grew "in wisdom and stature and in favor with God and men" (2:52). Luke did not try to explain how the divine and the human are related in Jesus Christ. But he did present him at the outset as "Son of God" (1:35) and as one who grew as a man grows (2:40,52). In the closing verses of the Gospel, Jesus is presented as one who could be handled (24:39) and who ate a broiled fish (24:42) and also as one who was worshiped (24:52).

At the Temple, Mary learned something more of the sword which was to pierce her heart (2:35). For Jesus to accept the claims of his Father's house meant the leaving of Mary's house. Jesus continued for many years to live in his mother's home, obedient to earthly parental authority; but he was obedient to a higher claim which she poorly understood. She did not begin really to find him until she seemingly had lost him.

3

Special Preparation for Public Ministry

3:1 to 4:13

THE MINISTRIES OF John the Baptist and Jesus were closely linked, and for a time they paralleled one another. However, the word of God came to John (3:2); and apparently it was through the preaching of John, at least in part, that Jesus responded to the call of God. John the Baptist was an important figure at the outset of Jesus' ministry.

To recognize the role of John the Baptist in the life of Jesus in no way reflects negatively against Jesus. The humanity of Jesus was as real as was the deity. John rightfully "decreased" as Jesus "increased," but John played an important role in the early ministry of Jesus. John baptized Jesus, and some of the earliest followers of Jesus were first disciples of John. Jesus, who was truly man as well as the one in whom God himself came uniquely, *grew*. One who was born into the world as an infant came to an understanding of the uniqueness of his person and mission as the Son of God. He read the Scriptures, and he also heard the word of God as it came through John the Baptist.

The call that came to Jesus was to summon him from the peace of his Nazareth home into a ministry of suffering service which would take him to the cross and to the glory beyond. In this section of Luke's Gospel John looms large, but he gave way to the one whom he baptized. John's preaching was caught up in the preaching of Jesus and in Jesus reached its fulness and finality.

29

I. THE MINISTRY OF JOHN (3:1-20)

1. *The World Setting* (3:1-2)

Luke introduced the ministry of John, and thus of Jesus, in a world setting. This is in keeping with Luke's theme of a gospel to all nations. Tiberius Caesar succeeded Augustus, who died August 19, A.D. 14. Tiberius was associated with Augustus for two years (A.D. 12-14), but he was not recognized as emperor until the death of Augustus. Accordingly, the fifteenth year of Tiberius would have been about A.D. 28-29. Pilate was the Roman procurator (governor) of Judea and Samaria, A.D. 26-36. Herod Antipas, son of Herod the Great, was tetrarch of Galilee and Perea, 4 B.C.–A.D. 39. Philip, his half brother, was tetrarch of Iturea and Trachonitis, 4 B.C.–A.D. 33 or 34. The identity of "Lysanias, tetrarch [ruler] of Abilene," is not clear. There was a well-known Lysanias who ruled in this area in 40 B.C., long before the time Luke is describing. However, there are two existing inscriptions which seem to point to a second Lysanias in the time of Tiberius.

Mention of two high priests, Annas and Caiaphas, seems strange when one remembers that the high priesthood was supposed to have been for life. The record in Luke is correct; for Annas had held the office in A.D. 6-15 and continued to have great influence although Caiaphas, his son-in-law, held the office in A.D. 18-36. Five sons of Annas held the office, four before and one following Caiaphas. Since the time of the Syrian king Antiochus Epiphanes (175-164 B.C.), the high priesthood had been degraded and corrupted as greedy men sought it. In turn, Syrian and Roman rulers appointed and deposed high priests at will as they yielded to bribery or as it suited their political interests. Annas and Caiaphas belonged to a long line of corrupt and often brutish high priests. It was in such times that "the word of God came to John the son of Zacharias in the desert" (3:2).

2. *The Word of God* (3:3–6)

The word of God came to John, seized him, and sent him forth into the regions around the Jordan River, "preaching a repentance-baptism unto [or on the basis of] the forgiveness of sins" (3:3). God's word is not only a teaching to be discussed or an idea which man embraces. It is also an event or occurrence which grasps men in the course of life. God's word, when it comes, does not compel men to the point of usurping personal freedom. But its very character is so demanding that men give themselves to it willingly.

3. *The Preaching of John* (3:7–20)

John preached a "baptism of repentance." He immersed in water those who gave evidence of repentance. He turned away those who came without "fruits worthy of repentance" (3:8). Baptism was the outer sign for the radical change to which John called the people. John was a prophet; and, like many of the prophets of old, he used a dramatic sign or "acted parable." In the dramatic sign "the repentant sinner was submerged, drowned as it were, to mark the end of the old life" (Browning). Water was used in various Jewish rites before and including John's time. Possibly his baptism was an adaptation of some older rite, giving it new content. The Qumran community near the Dead Sea (probably Essene) seems to have practiced immersion, but its exact nature is not clear. Proselytes to Judaism—Gentile converts—were immersed in water, in addition to the requirement of circumcision for men and the offering of a sacrifice required of all. Jewish proselyte baptism was probably pre-Christian, but this is not certain.

Repentance in New Testament usage means more than "change of mind," although that is the literal meaning of the Greek word. The idea is that of conversion, a turning to God. It involves contrition and sorrow over one's sins and the confession of sins. John regarded baptism as meaningful only if it was based upon repentance. The phrase in verse 3 may be translated "unto the forgiveness of sins" or "on the basis of the forgiveness of sins." A parallel Greek construction is used in Matthew 12:41, where it is said that Ninevites "repented at the preaching of Jonah." However translated, the passage teaches that repentance and not baptism itself opens the way to forgiveness. Had John believed that baptism has power in itself to save, it would have been proper to have baptized all who came. Instead, he turned away many, demanding first that they show evidence of repentance (v. 8).

John preached a gospel, good news of salvation; but it was bound up with judgment upon sins (3:9). He proclaimed God's coming to mankind with the gift of salvation, but he also proclaimed God's demand upon man. John spelled out what he meant by "fruits worthy of repentance." He meant integrity in one's dealing with other people and active concern for their needs—giving a coat to a person who is without one (3:11), exacting no more than is due from a debtor (3:13), and refusing to use one's advantage over another to exhort from or intimidate him (3:14). To John, these were the signs of genuine repentance.

John denied that he was the Christ. His function was to baptize in water, calling men to repentance. The mightier one who was to come would baptize in or with the Holy Spirit and fire (3:16). Mark's Gospel is older than Luke's, and it has the simpler reading: "He will baptize you in the Holy Spirit" (Mark 1:8). This is also the reading in Acts 1:5 and 11:16. Luke's addition of "fire" seems to point to judgment. This is clearly the case in his reference to the "winnowing shovel" in the next verse (3:17). The shovel was used to throw the grain against the wind so that the chaff might be blown away. It was in this manner and with this content that John "preached the gospel" (3:18). The day of Messiah was a day of judgment to the proud but the day of salvation to the humble and fearful.

John saw that the preservation of the nation of Israel was no necessity with God, for God could create a new people or "new Israel" (3:8). The Christ would "sift" and "purge" the nation (3:16–17), creating a cleansed people for himself. Ties of flesh were not enough, even though one were a descendant of Abraham (3:8). This did not please those who thought that the Christ would take the side of Israel against the Gentiles. John did not spare even the Jewish rulers. He condemned as illicit the marriage of Herod Antipas to his brother's wife (3:19). This led to John's arrest and finally to his execution (3:20; 9:9).

II. Jesus' Response (3:21 to 4:13)

1. *His Baptism* (3:21–22)

That Jesus was baptized by John is not open to doubt. The church would never have invented this; but the church did have to explain why Jesus submitted to John for baptism, especially in view of the fact that John baptized sinners. Matthew quoted Jesus as saying that his concern was "to fulfil all righteousness" (3:15). Submitting to baptism was not merely an accommodation to John—it was a right thing to do. Jesus thus humbled himself; and, though sinless, he took his place among the sinners from whom he would demand and to whom he would offer righteousness. Through Jesus' baptism, temptation, and descent from Adam, Luke shows Jesus' identification with mankind.

In describing Jesus' baptism, Luke stressed outward signs. The Spirit is represented as coming upon Jesus as a dove. This may be reminiscent of Genesis 1:2, where the Spirit of God was seen as brooding on the waters. Jewish rabbis had compared this movement of the Spirit to the brooding of a dove.

The voice which came to Jesus in his baptism is highly significant: "Thou art my beloved son; in thee I am well pleased" (3:22). This may echo both Psalm 2:7 and Isaiah 42:1, the word "son" coming from the Psalm and the rest from Isaiah. The center of Jesus' understanding of himself and his role seems to have been his awareness of God as his Father. This is seen both at his baptism (3:22) and on the occasion of his visit to the Temple at the age of twelve (2:49). Psalm 2 and Servant passages of Isaiah (42:1–4; 49:1–6; 50:4–11; 52:13 to 53:12)[1] seem to have given direction to his thought about himself. He saw himself as God's Son in a unique sense. He also saw that it was in suffering service that he was to fulfil his calling. Psalm 2 spoke of the Son as also God's anointed (Christ). His work would be to enable men to know God as their Father and to accept his sovereign rule in their hearts.[2] Isaiah 42:1 pointed to the role of suffering service.

The followers of Jesus stumbled over the idea of a suffering Messiah. The prevailing messianic expectation among the Jews was one which saw him in the likeness of David. He would destroy the enemies of Israel and restore Israel to her proper glory. That he would suffer humiliation, rejection, betrayal, and death was unthinkable to those who expected a Davidic type of Messiah. Jesus accepted the term Christ, but it required interpretation. His favorite self-designation was "Son of man," drawn seemingly from Daniel

---

[1] The Servant in Isaiah is one who suffers redemptively. He is God's Servant, and through him God redeems his people. At first the Servant may have been identified with Israel or a remnant within Israel, but finally the Servant proves to be one individual, Jesus Christ.

[2] William Manson, *The Gospel of Luke,* (New York: Harper & Row, 1930), p. 32. For a study of Jesus' self-understanding, see William Manson, *Jesus the Messiah;* J. W. Bowman, *The Intention of Jesus* (Philadelphia: Westminster Press, 1943); and E. A. McDowell, *Jesus and His Cross* (Nashville: Broadman Press, 1944), formerly published as *Son of Man and Suffering Servant.*

7:13. Both titles should be interpreted in terms of the Suffering Servant in Isaiah and Zechariah (9:9).

2. *His Genealogy* (3:23-38)

Luke traced the lineage of Jesus back to Adam, thus relating him to all humanity. This is one of many ways in which Luke's Gospel presents "the gospel to all people." Jesus was the Christ, the hope of Israel; but he was also the Son of man whose concern was to bring all nations under the sovereign rule of God. Adam represents the unity of the human race, stronger than its differences.

Luke and Matthew both trace the lineage of Jesus through Joseph, the legal but not actual father of Jesus. Luke's "as was supposed" (3:23) is his way of reminding the reader that the tracing of the genealogy through Joseph does not conflict with the divine origin or virgin birth of Jesus. Legal sonship was recognized through Joseph.

There are many unsolved problems which arise out of a comparison of the genealogies in Matthew and Luke. In Matthew, for example, Joseph is the son of Jacob, but in Luke of Heli. Matthew traced the line through David's son Solomon, but Luke traced it through David's son Nathan. It is best to conclude with William Manson that we do not know enough of the sources to make further discussion fruitful. To become absorbed in such problems is to miss the theological interests of Matthew and Luke. Matthew's genealogy is pointed up in such a way as to stress the fact that Jesus Christ is "son of David, son of Abraham" (1:1), and thus is the one in whom the covenant promises with Abraham and David are filled. Luke's theological interest is served in pointing out the organic relationship of Christ with all humanity, and thus is served Luke's purpose of demonstrating a gospel to all people.

Jesus was about thirty years of age when he began his public ministry. Some translations confuse Luke's statement, having it that "Jesus himself began to be about thirty years of age." The idea is, "Jesus, beginning his ministry, was about thirty years of age." Thirty is a round number, not an exact one. It is impossible to ascertain the exact age of Jesus or the time of his birth, although all evidences point to his birth shortly before the death of Herod the Great (4 B.C.).

3. His Temptations (4:1–13)

That Jesus was actually tempted is well attested in the New Testament. The writer of Hebrews affirmed that he was tempted in all things as are we, but that he did not sin (4:15). These were real temptations, not "straw men" or sham battles. The humanity of Jesus was taken seriously by the New Testament writers. Jesus was not only sinless; he was righteous. This righteousness was his own achievement under conditions of severe and repeated trials and temptations.

It is significant that the very writers, Matthew and Luke, who tell of the miraculous conception of Jesus are also the ones who give most attention to Jesus' temptations. They do not credit his sinlessness to Mary as is done in much theology. As early as the second century, the victory over sin was being found in Mary herself. The dogmas of her "immaculate conception" and her "perpetual virginity" are well-intended but misguided efforts to account for the sinlessness of Jesus by seeing Mary herself as sinless. This is foreign to the New Testament. Jesus was tempted even as we are tempted, but he triumphed where we have failed.

The particular temptations which followed the baptism of Jesus relate directly to his work as the Christ. The questions faced in them had to do with the nature of his mission and how it was to be accomplished. What kind of Messiah was he to be? Was he to use his powers for himself? Was he to tempt God by creating situations designed to force God to act in his behalf? Was he to "prove" God's faithfulness? Was he to let important but secondary values like bread become primary? Or was he to trust God absolutely, obey him absolutely, and seek to glorify God alone?

Jesus saw himself as Messiah and accepted the title, but he rejected current understandings of Messiah. He refused to be a political Messiah, taking Israel's side against the Romans and fighting for material gains. He would establish his kingdom through a cross, not a sword; and by giving life, not by taking it.

The first temptation was to turn stones into bread (4:3–4). Jesus was hungry, and he lived in a land filled with hungry people. Jesus was concerned that people have bread (all four Gospels tell of the feeding of the five thousand). He would not feed himself, but he would feed five thousand! Men cannot live without bread. No person doubts this. But neither can man live by bread alone. This is a basic lesson and hard to learn. Jesus refused to anticipate for himself the bounty which the Father would provide in his own time and way. He refused to make selfish use of the power at his command. He also rejected a role that would have fulfilled popular messianic hopes. He could have satisfied the immediate physical needs of a people who lived in a land of which not more than one fifth was arable and which was often plagued by famine. Probably the basic lesson, however, is that Jesus refused "to satisfy himself of the truth of God's word by a test of his own" (Plummer).

The second temptation in Luke's narrative was to gain the kingdoms of the world by bowing down and worshiping the devil (4:5–8). (Matthew and Luke differ as to the order of the temptations. It is futile for us to attempt to determine the actual order.) It was a popular Jewish expectation that the Messiah would defeat Israel's enemies and restore to Israel a glorious kingdom such as she had enjoyed under David. Jesus would have had the nation at his feet had he accepted that kind of messianic role. Since 63 B.C., the Jews had been under the rule of the Romans. Except for a brief period of independence under the Maccabees (142–63 B.C.), they had been under bondage to some foreign conqueror since the exile: Babylonian, Persian, Greek (Ptolemaic and Syrian), Seleucid, and now Roman.

There were many of the Zealot movement, who posed as or were acclaimed Messiah, seeking to bring in the messianic kingdom through military might. Jesus repeatedly rejected this role. To have sought this kind of "messianic" kingship or to have used the world's means for gaining power would have been idolatrous, like worshiping the devil.

The third temptation was to put God to the test by leaping from the high wing or wall of the Temple in Jerusalem (4:9–12). (There was a Jewish tradition that the Messiah would appear suddenly in the Temple.) In thus "proving God," one would have no further need to walk by faith. The word for Temple (*hieron*) designates the total Temple area with all its courts and buildings, not the sanctuary proper (*naos*). The southeast corner of the wall overlooked the deep Kidron Valley. To jump from it, expecting God to send his angels to the rescue, would be presumption and not faith. Demand for "proof" from God is also the denial of faith. This is to tempt, not trust, God.

Thus all three temptations were messianic in nature; that is, they reflect popular Jewish understandings of the role of Messiah. To Jesus, committed to the will of God alone, these "messianic" ideas were not of God but of Satan. They represented the world's false hopes. The answer to all these temptations is a firm faith in the will of God, a will not to be forced, but to be trusted and obeyed. Jesus was concerned that God's will be trusted and obeyed and that God's work be done to God's glory. It may also be observed that the Scriptures are not to be used, as the devil sought to use them, but they are to be obeyed.

Part 3

MINISTRY IN GALILEE

Luke 4:14 to 9:50

ONE OF THE EARLIEST attempts to take the life of Jesus occurred in his home town and, of all places, in the very synagogue which he had attended as a child. It is proverbial that a prophet is not without honor except in his own country. This was a part of the problem, but there was more to it. Jesus' statements in a synagogue sermon in Nazareth aroused the congregation to such hostility that there was an attempt to murder Jesus. This incident and its implications contain the central message which unfolds in Luke's two volumes.

Part three of this study consists of two chapters and covers Luke 4:14 to 9:50. Galilee provides the geographical setting for this section of Luke. These chapters cover much of Jesus' ministry; for, beginning with 9:51, he is pictured as "going up to Jerusalem," where eventually he was crucified. These two chapters show how Jesus began his ministry within the Jewish synagogues and how he was forced out of them as certain controversial issues were raised.

Chapter four (4:14 to 6:11) presents the early ministry of Jesus begun in the synagogues. The nature of his ministry is shown, along with its reception. Next is portrayed the beginning of conflict between Jesus and the Pharisees. The causes of the conflict are spelled out. A fundamental conflict existed between what Jesus offered as messianic ministry and what was desired by the Jewish nation as a whole.

Chapter five (6:12 to 9:50) traces a ministry gradually

being forced outside the synagogues. Some contact was maintained with the synagogues, but this became increasingly difficult. Jesus called disciples to himself and began the formation of a new people. For the most part, they came from people who were not carefully observing the ritual law, not from the religious leadership. The true people of Christ are shown to be those hearing and doing God's will (8:21). Ultimately, it will be shown that worldly distinctions, like nationality or race, Jew or non-Jew, are not significant in God's sight.

4

Ministry Begun in the Synagogues

4:14 to 6:11

THERE IS A STRIKING CONTRAST between the opening and closing verses of this section. To feel the full force of it, the reader should turn to 4:14–15 and then to 6:11. In 4:14–15 one reads that when Jesus returned to Galilee, his fame spread throughout the whole region, and "he taught in their synagogues, being glorified by all." One reads in 6:11, "They were filled with madness, and they were discussing with one another what they might do to him." What happened? How did fame and glory give way to enmity and murderous attack?

This section will show Jesus' gradual movement away from his family and the institutional religion of the synagogue. It was not by his choice that Jesus moved away from them. He was rejected and pushed out. He found disciples in places least promising. He was rejected among those most favorably situated for accepting him. The Pharisees rejected Jesus chiefly because he did not honor the distinctions which they made between "the righteous" and "the sinners." Jesus looked upon all as sinners and offered the same salvation to all.

I. Rejected at Nazareth (4:14–30)

This section gives the keynote for both the Gospel of Luke and Acts. The Nazareth incident actually took place later in the ministry of Jesus, as 4:23 implies. But Luke placed it here as a "frontispiece," or introduction, because it is

41

related to what he wished to develop in the two volumes, Luke-Acts. Luke depicted Jesus as God's Anointed who would bring salvation, not only to the Jews, but to all who would believe in him. Luke was concerned with Jesus' mission to the whole world and the relationship of Jewish rejection to that mission.

In his home synagogue in Nazareth, Jesus declared his understanding of himself and set forth the lines along which his ministry would move. The initial response was favorable, but it soon turned to anger and rejection. It was when Jesus spoke of a ministry beyond Israel, a ministry to Gentiles as in the times of Elijah and Elisha, that the synagogue became hostile toward him. They tried to destroy him, but he "passing through the midst of them proceeded on his way" (4:30). The story traced in Luke and Acts is that of rejection at home and acceptance from afar; rejection in Israel and acceptance among the Gentiles. To be more precise, it is the story of initial acceptance among the Jews followed by rejection when it became clear that Gentiles, too, were to be included in the new fellowship of Christ. Then, as now, the hardest demand was to accept all the people whom Christ accepted.

Jesus went into the synagogue on the sabbath by custom (4:16). Luke's Gospel shows that this turning point in the ministry of Jesus came as he moved "in the power of the Holy Spirit" (4:14). The mission which was to go beyond Israel into all the world was of God. It came through one who was faithful to true Judaism.

In the synagogue, Jesus was asked to read from and explain the Scriptures. It was normal procedure for the president of the synagogue to call upon some man in the congregation to render this service. Any adult male in the synagogue could be called on to do this. It was not a permanent or regular assignment, and it was an honor to be asked to read.

Jesus read from Isaiah (58:6; 61:1-2). This Scripture passage set forth the main lines of his ministry. He saw himself and his ministry described in these verses. As the "anointed" (Messiah or Christ) and with the Holy Spirit upon him, he was to preach the gospel to the poor. In Luke's Gospel the "poor" are not the materially poor alone, but the "poor in spirit" (Matt. 5:3). His work was to be characterized by release for captives, giving sight for the blind, liberation for those bruised (those shattered in fortune or broken in spirit), and proclamation of "the year of the Lord's favor" (Smith-Goodspeed). We should probably understand "the year of the Lord's favor" to mean the messianic age. Reference may be to the jubilee year of Leviticus 25:10–17. Jesus' concern was with people, not with the institutions of religion like the sabbath, purification rites, and fasting. He was, and is, concerned for all the needs of the people—sight, hearing, food, forgiveness, and the fulness of life.

When Jesus claimed that this Scripture was being fulfilled among them that very day, they at first marveled at the graceful words from his mouth. Soon, however, they were reminding themselves that he was "Joseph's son." Their admiration was mingled with annoyance that such words came from one whom they had known as a boy in the neighborhood. The people of Nazareth wanted proof of his claim— some sign like the words reported from an earlier ministry in Capernaum (4:23). Their wonder gave way to doubt. Instead of faith as unconditional trust in God, they demanded proof by signs. Next, their doubt gave way to anger and murderous intent (4:28–29).

When Jesus reminded the people from their own Scriptures that God's prophets were often rejected at home (4:24) and that God had never limited himself to Israel, they became violent. Jesus reminded them that, in the time of Elijah, a widow in the land of Sidon had received God's blessing through the prophet at the very time that many in Israel suffered famine. He reminded them that, in the time of Elisha, it was Naaman, the Syrian, who was healed of leprosy when there were many lepers suffering in Israel.

This was too much for those who thought that they had prior claims on God. They arose in wrath, threw Jesus out of the synagogue, and tried to kill him. That was some turn for a sabbath service! Jesus was rejected by the leading religious people of his nation. They were determined to destroy him, not because he claimed to be the Christ, but because he dared to interpret the messianic work as involving all the needs of all the people, within and beyond the nation Israel. He would make no significant distinction between Jews and Gentiles.

Jesus was rejected in the synagogue; but he, "going through their midst, proceeded on his way" (4:30). This in brief is the story told in Luke's Gospel and Acts. The glorious triumph attained in extending the gospel to all the people of the world was attended by the indescribable tragedy of self-exclusion by the very people from whom Jesus came.[1] There are always people who want God on their own terms, but one cannot have God while rejecting God's people.

II. WHOM JESUS ACCEPTS (4:31 to 5:16)

Jesus was rejected by many in Nazareth. What of his own standards for acceptance and rejection of persons? Jesus offers himself to all people, but there are conditions under which he offers or withholds himself. Such fact is strikingly illustrated in this section. Jesus accepts those who know themselves to be unworthy of acceptance, and he rejects those who try selfishly to possess and use him.

Jesus' acceptance of a man possessed by a demon (4:31–37) illustrates his willingness to accept those who know themselves to be unworthy of acceptance. One such man cried out, "What do we have in common, Jesus the Nazarene

---

[1] See Stagg, *The Book of Acts, the Early Struggle for an Unhindered Gospel* for a development of this understanding of Acts.

... I know who you are, the holy one of God" (4:34). Jesus did not stand off from the man. Jesus freed him from the evil spirit by which he was bound.

The overcoming of demons was one of the messianic expectations. Jesus came into a world which lived in the fear of demons. It was a part of Jesus' mission to destroy them (4:34). Christians today know nothing of this fear once prevalent in the world—that one might swallow a demon in drinking a glass of water or that to dig into a mountain might arouse a hostile demon. Modern science and medicine would be impossible had our world not been freed of the fear of demons. Whatever is to be made of demons, the coming of Jesus into the world has resulted in a situation radically different from that which he found. Probably the reader of these lines rarely, if ever, thinks of demons except when he reads about them. Jesus overcame the demons and turned attention from them to the evils within the human heart and mind. These, too, he can overcome. He will overcome them for those humble enough to acknowledge their need and accept his help.

A second illustration of the basis upon which Jesus accepts people is seen in a wonder of grace at the Lake of Gennesaret (Galilee), more wonderful even than that of a miraculous catch of fish (5:1-11). Simon Peter and other fishermen had fished all night and caught nothing. Jesus gave them a catch of fish so great that it nearly sank two boats. More amazing yet was Jesus' acceptance of a self-confessed sinner and the enlistment of this sinner in Jesus' great work of fishing for men.

In the presence of Jesus, Peter was so smitten with a sense of his own sin that he cried out, "Depart from me, for I am a sinful man, Lord" (5:8). Peter knew that as a sinner he had no right to Christ's presence. But Christ in his mercy does not send away the contrite sinner; he draws the sinner close to himself and even into his service. It is out of such people that he builds his church. (See 5:32.) Out of such he makes "fishers of men."

A third illustration that Jesus accepts those considered unacceptable is that of the cleansing of a man full of leprosy (5:12–15). Lepers were expected to cry "unclean" whenever approached by other people, thus to warn against defilement. A corpse was the only thing a Jew considered more defiling than leprosy. The leprosy of the Bible was a skin disease, but it was not the disease known today by that name. Jesus *touched* a man "full of leprosy" (5:12–13)! He touched the "untouchable."

But there is a less happy side to this issue. Jesus rejected some people who came to him—those who sought selfishly to possess and use him. He withdrew from the crowds which tried to retain him for themselves so that they could enjoy the benefits of physical healing. Jesus was concerned to heal the sick, but he did not want to build a following as a miracle worker. Furthermore, he refused to let any individual or community possess him to the exclusion of others (4:40–44). Neither then nor now does Jesus offer himself to those unwilling freely to share him and his redemptive message with others. (See Matt. 10:8.)

III. CONFLICT WITH THE PHARISEES OVER THE NATURE OF RE-
    LIGION (5:17 to 6:11)

Jesus' willingness to accept all persons aroused strong opposition from the Pharisees. In fact, he and they were far apart in their approach to religion. Jesus was concerned about God and persons, first of all. The Pharisees were preoccupied with religion itself, with religion for its own sake: circumcision, the sabbath, purification rites, food laws, fasting, and the like. They considered themselves to be righteous and all who failed to observe their standards to be sinners. In this section, Luke pointed up the conflict between Jesus and the Pharisees over the authority to forgive sins, association with people outside the approved group, fasting, and the sabbath.

1. *Conflict over Forgiving Sins* (5:17–26)

Friends of a paralytic had such faith and concern for their friend that they found a way to Jesus when the crowds at the door blocked their way to him. They went up to the housetop, presumably a flat roof accessible by an outside stair, and lowered the man through a hole made by removing tiles from the roof.

The surprise came when Jesus said, "Man, your sins have been forgiven you" (5:20). Why did Jesus begin with the man's sin instead of his paralysis? One reason may have been that this was the man's real problem. There was a Jewish saying, recorded in the Talmud, "No sick man is healed until his sins have been forgiven him." Probably, Luke's primary interest was to show that the authority of Jesus in religion begins with the forgiveness of sins. The Pharisees protested that only God could forgive sins, and they accused Jesus of blasphemy.

Jesus then posed a puzzling question, "Which is easier, to say, your sins have been forgiven you; or to say, arise and walk?" (5:23). Since the former cannot be outwardly confirmed or refuted, it may seem to be the easier. From another standpoint, it is easier to say, "Arise and walk," for people are more receptive to physical and material benefits than the forgiveness of sins. Jesus turned first to a more important matter, the forgiving of sin. He did heal the paralytic and also maintained his authority to forgive sins.

For the first time in Luke's Gospel, the term Son of man is employed (5:24). This was the favorite self-designation of Jesus. The term probably was taken over from Daniel 7:13, although some scholars believe it is derived from Ezekiel and some from the nonbiblical book of Enoch. In Daniel, the term designated a heavenly man who came upon the clouds and to whom was given a universal kingdom. In that kingdom, "all people, nations, and languages should serve him"; and the kingdom would never pass away (7:14). It seems that Jesus saw himself as the fulfilment of this picture in Daniel. As the Son of man, he would reign universally and eternally. At this point, it is the authority of the Son of man which is stressed. Later, Jesus will show that as Son of man he will fulfil his mission through suffering service. Jesus refused to be the Pharisees' kind of Messiah, one whose mission was to reward the "righteous." He came rather as the Son of man, offering salvation to sinners of all nations.

2. Conflict over Eating with Sinners (5:27–32)

Levi was a "tax collector," a more exact translation than "publican" as in the King James Version. The Romans retained direct responsibility in Palestine for collecting regular taxes, like land or poll taxes; but they farmed out to private contractors the collection of tolls from those who transported property by land or water. These offices were awarded by the Roman Government on the basis of competitive bids. Taxes were then collected on a commission basis. This opened the way for bribes and other offenses. Collaboration with Rome plus contact with Gentiles would add to the stigma of the office. The "tax collectors" were especially hated. In the New Testament, "tax collector" may refer to the subordinates who actually did the collecting rather than to the contractors who bought the concession.

It was a bold move on the part of Jesus to include one like Levi in his inner circle. Levi was counted a sinner both in personal life and in his profession. To the Pharisees, he was an outcast. The Pharisees were the "separatists," this being the meaning of the name. Their separation was from what they considered "unclean"—including both things and people. "Pharisee" was the term by which they were called, but they called themselves "Haberim," that is, neighbors.

However, their "Haberim," or neighbors, were restricted to the Pharisees.

Jesus shocked the Pharisees and their scribes [2] by not only including Levi in his company but also by eating with "publicans and sinners" (5:30). It was in table fellowship that the Pharisees were strictest. For the Pharisees, piety made much of separation; and Jesus included the very ones whom the Pharisees were most concerned to exclude. Jesus rejected the superficial grounds upon which the Pharisees distinguished between the "righteous" and the "sinners." They based it on such things as descent from Abraham, circumcision, purification rites, food laws, and sabbath observance. Jesus based the distinction upon what one through repentance and faith had let God do in the innermost self. Jesus looked upon Pharisee and publican as sinners, both under the same judgment and requiring the same salvation. It was for this principle that he set about to create a "new Israel," a new people of God, without regard for nationality, race, or other distinctions of the world.

Jesus said, "I have not come to call righteous people but sinners to repentance" (5:32). His ministry was to sinners as a physician's is to the sick. In this, Jesus and the Pharisees were poles apart. To the Pharisee, salvation was a reward for righteousness, achieved mainly by separation from what he considered unclean. The synagogues stood open to repentant sinners, but the religious leaders did not seek out the sinners. Jesus *sought* sinners. Salvation is God's gift to sinners. Salvation is God's work, not man's. But the salvation which God offers is not mere indulgence. When God saves sinners, he does a creative work, giving man not only a new standing but a new kind of life. Jesus entered into fellowship, including table fellowship, with those most despised

---

[2] The scribes originally were those who copied the Scriptures, and then they became the recognized interpreters. Most scribes apparently were Pharisees.

by the Jewish religion of his day. There is little wonder that he was crucified! A major problem has always been that of accepting those whom Christ accepts. Many desire to accept Christ as they understand him or would like to imagine him to be. Fewer are willing to receive all whom he receives, regardless of worldly distinctions such as class, nationality, and race.

3. *Conflict over Fasting* (5:33–39)

Jesus and the Pharisees were in conflict over fasting. The Day of Atonement was the only fast required of the Jews by the Old Testament (Lev. 16:29). The Pharisees made it a mark of special piety to fast twice a week (18:12), on Monday and Thursday. This was in keeping with the tradition that Moses went up into Mount Sinai on Monday and returned on Thursday. The Pharisees were critical of any Jew who did not observe these days of fasting. Jesus fasted on occasion, but his fasting was not governed by a calendar. He fasted in times of crisis or deep concern, as following his baptism (4:2). He expected that his disciples would fast, but only as it was a spontaneous abstention, reflecting sorrow or concern. He illustrated his point by saying that the friends of the bridegroom fast after he has gone, not while he is present with them (5:35). Jesus had no use for fasting designed to impress other people or God.

Jesus likened himself to a bridegroom, and in this he implied that the religion which he offers is one of joy. Messianic times were expected to be times of joy. Reference to the bridegroom's being taken away apparently refers to Jesus' death. The note of joy is all the more significant in view of the fact that Jesus was willing to endure the cross for the joy it would make possible. (See Heb. 12:2.)

In the parables of the patched garment (5:36) and the new wine (5:37–38), Jesus indicated his refusal to limit the religion of life to old forms and customs. To patch an old garment with a piece of new, unshrunk cloth would be to damage the old garment. To put new wine in old, brittle skins would be to lose both wine and skins; for as the wine fermented it would break the skins. (Glass bottles were unknown or unused because of expense, and the skins of animals were made into bottles. New skins would stretch, but old ones would not.)

Specifically, Jesus meant that he would not impose things like fasting, food laws, and sabbath observance upon his disciples. His purpose was to give life in abundance, not to diminish it. He came to create a fellowship of persons under the kingdom or sovereign rule of God, not to make men slaves to religious systems. As new wine requires fresh skins (5:38), so would the new life he offered require expressions of worship, fellowship, and service suited to its nature.

In 5:39, the preference of the old to the new, Jesus pointed to man's reluctance to change. Man often is more impressed with the antiquity of a religious practice than with its validity. Jesus offers freedom from the shackles of religion in favor of the freedom of the religion of the Spirit.

4. Conflict over the Sabbath (6:1–11)

The sabbath was a major area in which the basic conflict between Jesus and the Pharisees became evident. The Pharisees put the day above man; Jesus put man above the sabbath. The Pharisees had expanded the Old Testament commandment about the sabbath. There is an entire chapter in the Mishnah (rabbinic law) which deals with the regulations of the sabbath. There was a rule for almost every possible question pertaining to sabbath observance: how far one might walk on the sabbath, how much weight he might lift, whether or not one might eat an egg which had been laid on the sabbath. Jesus not only refused to observe these rules, he seems deliberately to have challenged them. His concern was to liberate man from all tyranny, including that of religion which had been made a burden to be borne rather than a power to sustain man.

Plucking grain and rubbing off the husks were acts which the Pharisees equated with harvesting and threshing. Jesus defended his disciples for doing these things. He based his defense on two considerations: human need and his own authority. David ate the loaves of shewbread when he was hungry, even though normally it was reserved for the priests. As Son of man, Jesus claimed to be Lord of the sabbath.

On another sabbath, Jesus healed a man who had a withered hand. He did it openly and boldly under the watchful eyes of the Pharisees. He condemned a "do-nothing sabbath," holding that on the sabbath it was lawful to do good, to save life. Not to do good or save life would be to harm or destroy life (6:9). Jesus made unmistakably clear his elevation of man above the sabbath, and because of this the Pharisees began to plot against him (6:11).

5

Ministry Outside the Synagogue

6:12 to 9:50

JESUS GREW UP among Jewish people who were faithful to synagogue and Temple. It was there that both he and his early disciples were accustomed to worship. But it was not in the settings of such worship that Jesus called his disciples. Boats and fishing nets and a tax collector's "place of toll" provided the setting for the calling of the twelve.

Jesus drew to himself many people who would have presented a strange appearance to one conditioned by the standards and patterns of the synagogue. Tax gatherers and Zealots were among the twelve, and his table companions included people referred to as "publicans [tax gatherers] and sinners." Jesus chose these people and claimed them as his own. Yet, it does not follow that he rejected the people of the synagogues. Many of them rejected him.

Thus far in Luke's Gospel there has been described the self-revelation of Jesus and the people's rejection of him. Now we begin to see the formation of a new people built around the twelve apostles. As Jesus moved deeper into his mission, indicating his intention more clearly by action and by words, it became increasingly apparent that he would be rejected by many and accepted by few. (Even the few who accepted only partly understood him.) Jesus was driven further from the established religion of the Jews. He found some acceptance by Jewish people inside and outside the synagogue and by Gentiles.

53

Alongside the story of his rejection is the story of the building of a group around Jesus himself. Jesus called twelve disciples to become his inner circle. These experienced many struggles in their effort to understand their Master. John the Baptist was puzzled by the way Jesus went about his ministry. In his transfiguration, Jesus faced his coming death and only Moses and Elijah were able to converse with him about it. Even at this late date, the disciples were competing among themselves for honors and expressing prejudice against those outside their group.

I. THE CHOOSING OF THE TWELVE (6:12–16)

The twelve men whom Jesus chose formed the nucleus of a new congregation of people. Probably the number twelve is significant, suggesting a "new Israel." The very fact that Jesus traveled about with twelve disciples could hardly fail to remind the people of the twelve patriarchs of Israel.

Although Jesus clearly came to call men to himself and to create a new community, he did not prefer to set up a group outside the synagogues and Temple. Had there been a different response to him, including the willingness to admit non-Jews—"publicans and sinners"—he may have been able to accomplish his purpose within existing Jewish structures. The book of Acts shows that for some decades Christian missionaries like Paul continued to worship and work through the synagogues and the Temple. But sharp conflicts with synagogue leaders drove out Jesus and, later, his followers.

That Jesus did appoint twelve apostles is well attested. Paul knew about "the twelve" (1 Cor. 15:5), and he felt it necessary to defend himself against unfavorable comparisons with the apostles (1 Cor. 9:1-2; Gal. 1:1,11; 2:6-9). The church would not have invented Judas and placed him among the trusted inner circle of Jesus. Although we know almost nothing about the majority of the twelve, with some uncertainty about the names of some of them, there is no reason to doubt that Jesus did appoint twelve of his followers to be apostles.[1]

The apostles are important chiefly because of their witness to Jesus (see Acts 1:21-22). They were called to be with Jesus and then were sent forth to preach (Mark 3:14). The basic witness contained in the New Testament is that of the apostles. When Christians in the early centuries sought out the writings which were to become canonical, they favored those which were thought to be directly or indirectly from apostles. The apostles were not rulers of the church. They were leaders, and preaching was their main function.

The "Sermon on the Plain" is a summation of what Jesus taught and of what the twelve were to teach. However, it does not necessarily follow that all of the sermon was directed only to the twelve. There is much in these teachings of Jesus for all his disciples.

II. TEACHING THE DISCIPLES: THE SERMON ON THE PLAIN (6:17-49)

There are close parallels as well as differences between the sermon in Luke and that in Matthew 5-7. It is pointless to argue whether they are two versions of the same sermon or two separate sermons, one from a mountain (Matt.) and one from a plain (Luke). To all appearances, both Matthew and Luke exercised liberty in giving topical arrangement to sayings and actions which they traced back to Jesus. This is not a weakness of either Gospel, for their interests were theological and not chronological. The concern of both was to present Jesus in terms of his origin, identity, gifts, and

---

[1] See Stagg, *The Book of Acts*, pp. 40ff., 101ff., for the understanding that the majority of the twelve dropped out of the biblical story because they never entered into the world mission to which they were commissioned. There are legends like the one which holds that Thomas carried the gospel into India. These legends may be true, but they have no biblical support.

demands. Maintaining the exact sequence or order of events and sayings was not essential to their purpose.

The sermon is heavy in its demands, so heavy that one feels overwhelmed by it. It is to be observed that the sermon is in a setting of mercy. Before and following the sermon, Luke (as did Matthew) told of merciful acts of healing. God's gifts come before his demands. The deliverance from Egypt preceded the law of Sinai. Salvation is both God's gift and his demand. Christians dare not forget either truth.

What one should look for in the "Sermon on the Plain" is not a complete sermon as originally delivered, but a close-up look at the teaching of Jesus as it sets forth the nature, privileges, and demands of Christian discipleship. The sermon in Luke falls into three parts: (1) introductory blessings and woes (6:20–26); (2) ethical principles (6:27–45); and (3) a concluding parable of judgment (6:46–49). These sections may be further divided, as follows.

1. Four Beatitudes (6:20–23)

These four beatitudes point to the reversal of values which will occur in the "age to come," the new order ushered in by the Messiah. In Jesus, this new age had arrived. Jesus was not saying that the poor are blessed because they are poor, but because theirs is the kingdom of God (see Matt. 5:3). It is so also with those who hunger, weep, and are persecuted. Their blessedness is that they will be filled and be joyful, and that they are in the company of the true prophets. The poor are assured that theirs is the kingdom of God. "Poor" had come to designate not only material poverty but religious piety.

Material poverty as such is not a blessing, and simply to be poor does not assure one of salvation. Material wealth does tend to give a false security (see 18:24–25), while the poor may more easily sense their dependence upon God. (By Palestinian standards of the first century, almost every

American today is rich.) Those who hunger and weep are assured not simply of a world to come in which all needs are met in a joyful state, but that in Christ life is filled with meaning even now. The "separation" of 6:22 probably is a reference to exclusion from the synagogue. Jesus taught that exclusion by religious people will be more than compensated for as one finds himself accepted by God. The Gospels repeatedly show Jesus identifying with the excluded (publicans, sinners, lepers) and not with the excluders (proud, self-righteous religious leaders).

2. Four Woes (6:24–26)

Four woes stand over against the four beatitudes and help interpret them. Neither beatitudes nor woes should be considered out of context. Those who hoard wealth in the midst of poverty, those who fill their own stomachs while others about them are hungry, and those who laugh in the midst of sorrow will ultimately experience the opposite. The teaching here parallels that of Matthew 25, where one's true attitude toward Christ is shown to be reflected in his attitude toward the hungry, the sick, and the friendless.

The false prophet shapes his message to suit the times. He basks for a time in the world's praise, but he and his message must ultimately be rejected. It is folly to seek the approval of sinful men only to fall under the judgment of God.

3. The Command to Love (6:27–36)

Can love be commanded? Can one will to love? Jesus taught precisely this. Love as he taught it is not a mere sentiment or emotion, awakened or snuffed out by forces and factors outside us. Love is a disposition, governed by factors within a person, including his will. It is the disposition to relate oneself to another for that one's good, regardless of cost or consequence to oneself. This love is the fruit produced by the Holy Spirit in a human life (Gal. 5:22). God is love, his love is self-sacrificing; it is self-giving. It is not the love that takes and uses; it is the love that gives and creates.

Love is not motivated by the goodness or beauty of the other. It seeks to bring about goodness and beauty in others. Love gives precisely because it is love. It is indiscriminate in that it seeks to bestow goodness or value regardless of the merit of the other. In this way, one shows himself to be God's child (6:35), seeking to do good for enemies as well as for friends.

The demands of love are hard. One may turn the cheek either literally or figuratively. To leave oneself open for further insult or injury is a risk which the Christian is to take as he seeks to help others. One's motives may be misunderstood, or one may suffer materially or physically as the price of trying to serve others. One's natural disposition is to protect his own "rights" and to retaliate when those rights are encroached upon. Jesus' teaching that one should give his coat to the one who robs him of his cloak, that he give to the one who wants to borrow, and that he not seek to recover stolen goods sounds so radical to us that we want to tone it down or explain it away. Of course, Jesus does not mean that one exhausts his responsibility to others by simply yielding to them in all their demands. One is obliged to help sinners mend their ways, but that is another story. Here Jesus is concerned that his disciples be freed from the self-centeredness which seeks to secure one's own rights. He is concerned that his disciples be governed by the love that seeks the good even of one's enemies. Love and mercy are to be expected in God's children, for God is like that.

4. *On Judging Others* (6:37–38)

To judge others in the effort to escape judgment will not work. One brings greater judgment upon himself this way.

Judgment is harsh upon one who judges harshly. The unforgiving person remains unforgiven because he is unforgivable. That is, the very condition which produces an unforgiving spirit is that which renders one unable to receive forgiveness. When one shuts another out, he shuts himself in. "Release and you shall be released!" (6:37). An unforgiving person is like a man who holds a bear by the tail—both man and bear are caught. How does one turn loose of the bear? He cannot do it without risk, but that is a risk he must take. Likewise, it is not easy to forgive or to accept forgiveness, but both to offer and to accept forgiveness are indispensable to the Christian life. They are painful but liberating. One who is unforgiving is imprisoned by his own wrong spirit. To forgive another is to find release for oneself. The stingy person lives in a stuffy little world. The generous person lives in a large world of light and life.

This section of Luke makes much of reward. It is important to see the nature of Christian reward. It is not set forth as motive for right conduct. It is not pay for merit or good works (see 17:9–10). Reward has to do with growth in character and life. Mercy, a forgiving spirit, and generosity yield a larger and freer life. Increased capacity for, and appreciation of, life are the rewards of the exercise of Christian attitudes and conduct. This is not to forget that the people of God may suffer material and physical want or even martyrdom. To follow Christ means, first of all, the acceptance of the way of the cross as the way of life. But this passage is saying that to a merciful and generous spirit life takes on new dimensions of freedom and meaning.

5. *Master and Disciple* (6:39–40)

Both master and disciple have responsibilities. A blind guide and his blind disciple will both fall in a ditch. It is foolish to follow a blind guide. It is the disciple's destiny to become like his teacher, as he is "completed" or "equipped" by his teacher (v. 40). An individual shares the destiny and character of the one whom he follows. The master is responsible for the guidance he gives, and the disciple is responsible for choosing the guide he will follow.

6. Mote and beam (6:41-42)

It would be ridiculous for a person with a beam (main support for floor or roof) in his eye to try to remove a speck from another's eye. Just so is it absurd for a sinner to try to deal with another's sin problem. He must be willing first to come under judgment for his own sin. It is only after the "beam" has been removed from one's eye that he can see clearly enough to help his brother. One does owe it to the other person to remove the "speck" from his eye. It is not to be a choice between "beam" and "speck." Both "beam" and "speck" are to be removed, in proper order. Christians are in the business of asking other people to undergo radical change; however, Christians must undergo change if they expect to change others. This does not mean that one must be perfect to help another. What is condemned here is the critical appraisal of others without awareness or acknowledgment of one's own faults.

7. Known by Fruit (6:43-45)

"Good" and "corrupt" fruit refer not to healthy and diseased fruit but to what is useful and worthless. "Good" and "corrupt" refer not to condition but to kind. A tree bears fruit according to its kind. John 15:1-17 and Galatians 5:22 are important parallels on the subject of fruit, and this fruit is not to be confused with mere results of human activity. By certain techniques and skills, or even by manipulation, man can produce certain overt results. But only the Spirit of God can produce "love, joy, peace, patience, kindness, goodness, faith [or fidelity], gentleness, and self-control" (Gal. 5:22).

8. *Two Foundations* (6:46–49)

Although one is saved by God's grace, he is judged by his works. Nothing short of obedience to God's Word is required. It is not enough to hear and to say, "Lord, Lord." One who does what God commands is like a man who builds upon a rock foundation. One who hears without doing is like a man building a house without a foundation. The New Testament teaches neither works without grace, nor grace without works. Salvation is God's work, not man's; but God saves by achieving in man a new quality of life.

III. JESUS' CONCERN FOR ALL PEOPLE (7:1–17; 7:36 to 8:3; 8:22–56)

The concern of Jesus for all people is seen most clearly in his relationship with outcasts, the sick, the sorrowing, and the helpless. By the time Luke wrote his Gospel and Acts, Christianity had reached deeply into the Gentile world. This outreach was foreshadowed in the ministry of Jesus to the rejected and neglected within Israel as well as to the Gentiles.

1. *Concern for a Gentile* (7:1–10)

A centurion, a soldier normally in command of a hundred men, caused Jesus to marvel; for he exercised such faith as Jesus had not found in Israel (7:9). Jesus saw the faith of this Gentile (vv. 5,9 imply that he was not a Jew) as being above that found in Israel. Thus was foreshadowed his rejection in Israel and acceptance among the heathen. The centurion counted himself unworthy, even though others called him worthy. He built his hope on the goodness and power of Jesus alone. That is our hope also.

2. *Concern for the Bereaved* (7:11–17)

Jesus' concern for others, regardless of danger or cost to himself, is forcefully illustrated in his touching the bier (open coffin) upon which a widow's son lay (7:11–17), even as he had touched a man full of leprosy (5:13). A corpse was considered even more defiling than a leper. In helping the leper and the widow, Jesus showed himself indifferent to his own security and concerned only for other people. He whose demands are so heavy, as seen in the Sermon on the Plain, was first of all one who came in mercy and to save. Jesus gives before he demands, and he gives more than he demands.

3. *Concern for a Sinful Woman* (7:36–50)

Jesus not only *touched* a leper and a dead man's coffin; he permitted a sinful woman to touch him (7:36–50). This took place in the home of a Pharisee, where Jesus was most vulnerable to attack by self-righteous and powerful religious leaders. A Pharisee named Simon had invited Jesus to dinner and then condemned him because Jesus permitted a sinful woman to touch him. The identity of the woman is unknown and unimportant. (The tradition that she was Mary Magdalene dates back to Gregory the Great, but this has no support in the narrative.) The woman had come to Jesus out of gratitude, bringing a flask of perfume, presumably to anoint him. At formal dinners, participants reclined on couches, their feet extending out from the table. Thus it was easy for the woman to stand over the feet of Jesus. Her outburst of tears was probably unanticipated by the woman; and as they fell upon Jesus' feet, she impulsively wiped them away with her hair. The whole act was spontaneous, an expression of love for one who was the "friend of publicans and sinners" (7:34). Jesus' concern for the sinful woman contrasted sharply with Simon's contempt for her.

Jesus' statement, "Her sins, which are many, are forgiven, for she loved much" (7:47), is as significant as it is difficult. She was not forgiven because she loved much. Her great love showed that she was conscious of having been forgiven much. Her faith had saved her (7:50); her love grew out of her gratitude for forgiveness. Love was the proof of forgiveness, not its ground. Self-righteous Simon had no love, for he had not known what it is like to feel rejected and then forgiven and accepted. The unmerciful and unforgiving show that they have not known what it is to receive mercy and be forgiven.

4. Concern for All Women (8:1-3)

Luke related that many women followed Jesus and ministered to him. More important than their identification is their presence. Jesus freed women from a merely sensual worth and from an arbitrary status fixed by their birth. In much of the first-century world, women were the property of men. Only men and boys participated in the synagogue services. The Jewish prayer book yet retains the prayer in which man thanks God that he is not an unbeliever, uncivilized, a woman, or a slave. This prayer can be traced back among the rabbis only to R. Jehuda ben Elaj (ca. A.D. 150), but it was a rather general proverb among Persians, Greeks, and Jews for some centuries before Christ.[2] The rabbis taught that it were better for the Law (Scriptures) to be burned than to fall into the hands of a woman.[3] It is only against this background that one can appreciate what Jesus did for women when he accepted them as persons with identity and dignity. One of Luke's purposes was to show the place Jesus gave women in his following. Whatever it may mean, no woman is mentioned in the Gospels as being hostile to Jesus.

---

[2] A. Oepke, "Woman," *Theological Dictionary of the New Testament,* tr. G. W. Bromily (Grand Rapids: Wm. B. Eerdmans, 1964), I, 777.

[3] *Ibid.,* I, 781.

5. *Concern for the Helpless* (8:22–56)

Luke brought together in this section four stories of man's helplessness and his hope: disciples saved in a storm on a lake (8:22–25); a demoniac made whole (8:26–39); the little daughter of Jairus raised up (8:41–42,49–56); and a woman healed of a twelve-year hemorrhage (8:43–48). The Lord who has power over nature, demons, death, and disease offers hope to the helpless. There is no person or human need beyond the concern of Jesus.

The concern of Jesus is most strikingly brought out by the contrast between the concern of Jesus to save a Gerasene demoniac and the concern of certain citizens over the loss of their hogs (8:26–39). Whatever the meaning of demons, the Gerasene was deranged, hostile, and possibly had a suicidal tendency. He was not one whole person; he was legion, fragmented into many. Jesus freed him from the demons; and the man was found clothed, in his right mind, and saved or made whole. "Saved" is used in various ways in the New Testament. Here it is used to refer to making a whole man well. Jesus is concerned not only for all men but for the wholeness of each man. In saving persons, Jesus is concerned to cleanse, heal, liberate, redirect, and empower them for a new kind of life. He is concerned to save man morally, spiritually, ethically, socially, and bodily.

IV. Varied Reactions to Jesus' Ministry (7:18–35; 8:4–18)

Jesus was "the Teacher" of all teachers, yet he often was misunderstood; and sometimes his teaching was rejected even when understood. The truth does not so overpower people as to be irresistible. It is often feared, resented, and rejected. Sometimes it is ignored because of indifference or because of preoccupation with something else. The truth is difficult to accept, even by those who desire it. To those who are indifferent or hostile, its acceptance is almost impossible. The chief reason many stumble over the teaching of Jesus is their unwillingness to accept his demands.

1. *The Problem of Hearing* (8:4–18)

The parable of the soils tells what ears are for but also shows that not all ears are hearing ones. There are as many responses to the gospel as there are responses of soil to seed. Some people are like a beaten path in a field, hard and impenetrable. Some are like the rocky ground where the soil is thin. These are the shallow or superficial ones who give easy response but no real commitment. Some are like the thorny ground with conflicting interests, the worldly interests winning out. Some are like the good soil—responsive and productive. Ears are to hear with, but some fail to hear either because of indifference, conflicting interests, or hostility.

Jesus spoke a most difficult word in saying, "To you it has been given to know the mysteries of the kingdom of God; but to the rest in parables, that seeing they may not see and hearing they may not understand" (8:10). If Jesus meant that understanding is arbitrarily withheld from some, then 8:18 remains hard to understand: "See then how you hear." However, Jesus insisted that the hearer is responsible for how he hears. Verse 10 does not mean that God determines who may understand and who may not. The difference is in the condition of the hearers. It has to do with attitude.

The conclusion to the parable is a warning that how one hears determines whether his capacity for hearing increases or decreases. This places the responsibility upon the hearer and not upon a fate imposed upon him. The one "who has" is the one receptive to the gospel. The one who "has not" is the one not open or receptive to it. The reward for openness to the gospel is greater capacity for it. The consequence of refusing to hear is the loss of ability to hear. Were God to determine the outcome, then he alone would be responsible for the result; and man would be relieved of blame. The force of the parable, therefore, is to place the hearers under judgment.

To some interpreters, this is the parable of the sower, not of the soils. They see it as designed to encourage, giving assurance that the word of God—the gospel—will triumph, whatever the opposition. There will be a harvest despite birds, rocky soil, and thorns. Verses 16 and 17 support this view. No man lights a lamp in order to cover it but to let it give light. God lights his lamps, and their light will be seen. He sows his seed, and there will be a harvest. However, as the parable stands in Luke's Gospel, it seems to be a warning or judgment upon the hearer of the word.

2. John's Uncertainty About the Coming One (7:18–30)

Even John the Baptist stumbled over the nature of Jesus' ministry. This limitation, along with the greatness of John, is clearly recognized (7:23,28). John wanted to understand Jesus, but neither he nor any other adequately understood the nature of the messianic ministry before the death and resurrection of Jesus. Jesus was not fulfilling John's understanding of the Messiah. There were "rotten trees" like Herod Antipas, but where was the "axe"? Where was the "winnowing shovel" and the separation of the "chaff" from the "wheat"? (See 3:9,17.) John had expected the overthrow of evil and the vindication of the right. Judgment and redemption would be open and decisive. Outwardly, however, nothing seemed to be changed. Herod Antipas was on his throne, and John the Baptist was in prison. John was uncertain, but he sought answer to his question from Jesus himself.

Basically, Jesus told John through his messengers that he would find his answer where he had found his question. The messengers were told to report to John what they saw and heard: Blind people were receiving sight; lame people were walking; lepers were being cleansed; deaf people were hearing; dead people were being raised; and poor people were being evangelized (7:22). The ministry thus described parallels that forecast in the Nazareth synagogue (4:18–19). Jesus' reply reflects Isaiah 29:18–19; 35:5–6; and 61:1. These passages witness to and support Jesus in the nature of his ministry.

The beatitude which followed is significant: "Blessed is he whoever shall not find occasion for stumbling in me" (7:23). The nature of Jesus' ministry was a stumbling block to many. He did not try to compel faith by outward signs. It disappointed Zealots who wanted the exaltation of Israel over other nations. It disappointed the Pharisees who wanted fulfilment of the Jewish law as they understood it, with stress upon ritual performance. Jesus' concern to meet all the needs of each person, physical and material as well as moral and spiritual, was not what was generally expected of the Messiah.

John's question was not secondary; it was the main one. Was Jesus the "Coming One," or was some other to be awaited? It is significant that Jesus did not reject John. He defended John against misunderstanding (7:24–28). John was no weakling, unwilling to suffer hardship. John's problem was not that he had to endure hardship. His problem grew out of the fact that he was not able to see how Jesus' ministry was fulfilling the role of Messiah, establishing the kingdom or rule of God, judging the wicked, and vindicating the righteous.

Jesus found none greater than John among those born of women; yet, John was declared less than the least in the kingdom of God (7:28).[4] John belonged to the old order,

---

[4] Some interpreters understand the comparison to be between Jesus and John, Jesus being the "lesser" in age and in years of ministry, yet the greater in the kingdom of God. Decision between this interpretation and the one above is difficult.

not the new. John stood at the end of a long line of prophets, but he died before the triumphant death and resurrection of Jesus. One today may have a better understanding of Christ than was possible for John, for now one may see him in the light of his greater victory. The least in the age of fulfilment is greater than the greatest in the age of preparation.

3. A Childish Generation (7:31–35)

Jesus found his generation to be childish, not childlike. A disciple is childlike, disposed to trust. The childish people rejected John because he was too austere and strict. They rejected Jesus because he seemed too much at home with the common people, especially those who today perhaps would be called "the unchurched." He did not observe the food laws, purification rites, or calendar days for fasting; and he was a friend of publicans and sinners. The religionists of Jesus' day were like spoiled children who refused to dance or to weep, to "play wedding" or to "play funeral." They did not know what they wanted and were dissatisfied with whatever was offered them.

The proverb in 7:35 is of uncertain meaning, "Wisdom is justified by all her children." Probably Jesus meant that his ministry would be validated by its outcome. Jesus aroused the hostility of many; and even his closest followers had serious misgivings about the way Jesus conducted his ministry, as is seen from their efforts to change it. Jesus was content to let the wisdom of his way be judged by what it produced.

V. JESUS REVEALS HIS TRUE MISSION (9:1–50; 8:19–21)

The more clearly Jesus emerged as the Servant of God who would give his life, the fewer the number who followed him. He reached the peak of his popularity when thousands followed for "the loaves and fishes," but they began to fall away from him as he gave himself to the way which led to his rejection and crucifixion. After a miraculous meal, more than five thousand wanted to make him king; but at the cross he hung between two thieves, and only a few faithful followers stood by. This is the story which already is unfolding in the section now under consideration.

Much is made today of "communication," as though human relationships would improve if we understood one another better. This is not necessarily true. Better understanding of one another may lead to further estrangement or division. According to the Gospels, Jesus was most popular when he was least understood. As he emerged more clearly, he was most feared and hated by some and abandoned by the masses. It continues to be true that Jesus is most "popular" when least understood—when made over into our own image. But he keeps coming back to us in his own character, judging us and sifting us. He wants the following of all, but never did he offer himself on our terms. Luke recorded some incidents which give us a clearer revelation of Christ's terms for discipleship.

1. The Feeding of the Five Thousand (9:11–17)

All four Gospels relate this story. Mark (6:45) and Matthew (14:22) tell us that following the feeding, Jesus forced the disciples into a boat and then dispersed the crowd. We have to turn to John's record to learn of the crowd's attempt to take Jesus by force and make him king (6:15). Luke omitted these details, but they show that the high point of Jesus' popularity was reached when he fed the five thousand. John's Gospel shows that the effort to make Jesus king, a political messiah, was rejected, although the twelve seemingly joined the crowd in the unsuccessful effort. Because Jesus refused to be their king-messiah, many turned back from following him (John 6:66).

2. Peter's Confession (9:18–27)

Verse 19 parallels verses 7–8, disclosing the multitude's conclusion that Jesus belonged to the prophets. This judgment contained a partial truth but was inadequate. Peter's confession, "the Christ of God," was much more adequate; yet it fell short. The apostles seem not to have thought beyond a political messiah who would restore Israel to her place of glory over the heathen nations (see Acts 1:8). Jesus accepted the title "Christ," but he went far beyond the twelve in interpreting it.

Son of man (9:22) was Jesus' favorite self-designation, according to the New Testament. Except for Stephen (Acts 7:56), no one called Jesus "Son of man" other than Jesus himself. "Son of man" was freer of abuse than was the nationally interpreted "Messiah," and it was richer in meaning. It designated a heavenly man to whom would be given a kingdom which was universal and unending. The "Son of man" would exercise judgment and would be identified with the saints of the most High God (Dan. 7:13–22).

What for the time was incredible to the apostles was Jesus' affirmation that the Son of man would suffer, be rejected by the Jewish leaders, and be killed. Jesus further demanded that any man who would come after him must take up his cross daily and follow him (9:23). Life could be known only through the strange way of the cross. To selfishly try to save life is to destroy it. To lose life for Christ's sake is to find it. Jesus further told the disciples that they would see the kingdom of God in their time. It would come, however, not on a wave of national triumph, but in the triumph of the cross.

3. The Transfiguration of Jesus (9:28–36)

Luke passed over Peter's protest concerning the death of Jesus; his transfiguration narrative brings out the disciples' slowness to accept the things Jesus said about his death. Only Luke recorded the subject of conversation when Moses and Elijah talked with Jesus. They spoke of "his decease [*exodos*] which he was to accomplish at Jerusalem" (9:31). The transfiguration served to strengthen Jesus for the ordeal which awaited him. It also served as instruction for the disciples, reluctant to consider the possibility of death for their Master. The voice which was heard proclaimed the truth brought out at the baptism of Jesus, "This is my Son, my chosen" (9:35; see 3:22). Added is the instruction sorely needed by the disciples, "Hear him!" According to Matthew, Peter had tried to instruct Jesus. He and his companions were to listen, in particular, to what Jesus had to say about the nature and means of his ministry.

4. *The Disciples' Pride and Prejudice* (9:37–50)

For lack of faith, the disciples were unable to help a man's epileptic son (9:37–42). The seriousness of their lack is further disclosed by their failure to understand Jesus' saying that the Son of man was to be delivered up into the hands of men (9:44). Luke wrote that the saying "was concealed from them that they should not understand it" (9:45). This does not mean that God was responsible for their not understanding. The strong language of verse 44 places the responsibility squarely upon the disciples: "Let these words sink into your ears" (RSV). They could have understood the warning about the cross had they been open to it.

The pride of the disciples is reflected in their quarrel about who among them was greatest (9:46). Their distorted idea about greatness shows that they had missed the point about "the Son of man who must suffer." With their pride was its ugly companion, prejudice (9:49–50). They boasted to Jesus that they had forbidden one not of their number to cast out demons in Jesus' name. Instead of the expected compliment, Jesus rebuked them, making room for this one who had not followed with them. Pride and prejudice and the unwillingness to hear reflect how little even the twelve understood Jesus as the Christ who was also the Son of man and the Suffering Servant.

5. *Jesus' True Family* (8:19–21)

Luke-Acts has as a major purpose the demonstration that God's people are those of faith, not of particular racial or national origin. In Christ, these worldly distinctions are insignificant. Those who think that they have special claims on Jesus because of who they are, claiming him as theirs to command and use, deny their only ground of hope. Jesus belongs to the one who says, "Depart from me, for I am a sinful man" (5:8). Jesus refused to limit himself to the special claims of some so that he might offer himself to all persons on terms possible of fulfilment by all.

Jesus made it clear that his true family is known not by ties of flesh, but by hearing and doing the word of God (8:21). Not even Mary and her children had special claims upon Jesus. The Gospel of Luke shows that Jesus had to deny the special claims of family, synagogue, and nation in order to give himself to the world.

Part 4

JOURNEYING TOWARD JERUSALEM

Luke 9:51 to 19:27

WHEN A STREAM widens out into a lake, it is difficult to detect the current, even though the lake empties into another stream on the farther side. Luke 9:51 to 19:27 is like such a lake. Although rich in content, both in terms of the deeds and words of Jesus, the organization of this section is not clear. It is hard to find its main "current," or line of progress.

Luke 9:51 may supply a clue to the leading idea of the section in the Greek word *analēmpsis*, "a receiving up." Although our Lord's ascension climaxed his "receiving up," Luke seems to view his rejection, crucifixion, and resurrection as included in the ultimate reception by the Father. His "way up" was by Jerusalem and the cross. Jerusalem, of course, was the place of his final rejection and crucifixion. Contrary to outward appearance, it was his victory, not defeat. Luke is somewhat like John's Gospel at this point in representing the death of Jesus as his glory.

Chapters six, seven, and eight of this book are organized around the theme "Journeying Toward Jerusalem." Readers of Luke are repeatedly reminded that Jesus is on his way to Jerusalem (see 9:51; 13:22; 17:11; and 19:28). It is not until 19:41 that Jesus actually reaches Jerusalem, but that destination is kept before the reader from 9:51 on. It is as though Luke let the shadow of the cross fall across this whole section. Luke made emphatic the cost to Jesus of his redemptive ministry and the cost of discipleship to those who would follow him. Along with the cost, we see God's joy in reclaiming the lost, the disciples' joy in following Jesus, and the assurance that God's triumphant kingdom is near.

6

Jesus' Face Set Toward Jerusalem

9:51 to 11:54

A WIDE RANGE of subjects is contained in the section of Luke covered by this chapter: Jesus' turning toward Jerusalem; the Jewish and Samaritan conflicts; Jesus' openness toward Samaritans; the sending of seventy disciples on a peace mission; meditation and prayer; the kingdom of God; and the judgment which falls upon the privileged.

I. GOING UP TO JERUSALEM (9:51–62)

Verse 51 registers a decisive turn in the ministry of Jesus: "When the days were being fulfilled that he should be received up, he resolutely set his face toward Jerusalem." It was there that he must finally press his claims upon his nation and call it to decision. He had been laying the necessary groundwork for this showdown in the capital city of Judaism. He had called a nucleus of disciples around which his new family was being built. He had given, in deed and word, basic instructions for the quality of life and ministry into which he called men.

There remained, however, the all-out call to his nation which could come only at its very nerve center—Jerusalem. Jesus knew well the risk of going there. The power structure of Judaism was there, represented by the Sanhedrin, made up of Sadducees and Pharisees. Jesus knew that rejection and death could await him. He wanted to save his nation, not alienate it; but he was prepared to face his people there, whatever the cost. He firmly set his face to go to Jerusalem.

1. Jewish and Samaritan Hostility (9:51-56)

Jewish and Samaritan hostility is reflected in the Samaritan's refusal to receive the Jewish disciples of Jesus and in the proposal of James and John that fire be called down from heaven to burn the Samaritans. This hostility dated back to the Babylonian exile, at which time the Samaritans rose as a mixture of Israelites and non-Israelites. Ill feelings were intensified when the returning Jews refused the Samaritan's offer to help rebuild the Temple at Jerusalem. The rupture between the two groups was almost finalized when John Hyrcanus, the Maccabean high priest and king, destroyed the Samaritan temple at Mount Gerizim (109 B.C.). It is strange that sinful people will not accept one another even though they ask God to accept them. Jesus rebuked the vengeful spirit of James and John. A Samaritan village rejected Jesus, but he did not reject the Samaritans.

2. Conditions of Discipleship (9:57-62)

The cost of discipleship is brought out in conversations with three would-be disciples (9:57-62). One volunteered to follow Jesus wherever he might go. Jesus was going to Jerusalem and the cross. Jesus warned the man that to follow him was to follow one who was rejected by the world. Foxes have dens and birds have nests, but Jesus had no place where he could rest in this world. Jesus did not mean that there was no home open to him. Many homes were open to him, like the home of Peter and that of Mary, Martha, and Lazarus. He meant that there was a basic conflict between himself and the world. A true follower of his would be caught up in the same conflict.

A second man wanted first to bury his father. Jesus demanded that his disciples give him first place, even ahead of family. Family ties were strong among the Jews, so the loyalty which Jesus required was to be the highest possible.

A third man wanted to put his house in order before following Jesus. Jesus told the man that there could be no looking back for his disciples and illustrated this by the plowman who must look forward if he is to plow a straight furrow.

II. THE MISSION OF THE SEVENTY (10:1–24)

The symbolic character of the number seventy is recognized by nearly all interpreters of this passage. According to Jewish reckoning, there were seventy nations in the world after the flood in the time of Noah (compare Gen. 10:32). The sending of seventy disciples dramatized the fact that the Gentiles were to be included in the new Israel which Jesus was forming. The appointment of seventy elders to serve under Moses may also be echoed in this passage (see Num. 11:16). (Some manuscripts read seventy-two instead of seventy. The Septuagint [Greek translation of the Old Testament] has seventy-two where the Hebrew has seventy for the nations in Gen. 10 and possibly for the elders in Num. 11:24,26. With either translation, the emphasis is on the symbolic nature of the number.) There are many evidences in Luke-Acts of Luke's emphasis upon the inclusion of Gentiles, Samaritans, and Jews in the family of God. Sending out the disciples "two by two" may reflect the principle of Deuteronomy 19:15, in which at least two witnesses were required for establishing a matter.

The picture of a great harvest and few laborers is a moving one (v. 2). It becomes more revealing when one recalls that there were thousands of religious workers, "clergy" and "laymen," in Palestine when Jesus prayed for workers. Religion was outwardly robust, but the people were being neglected in a religious situation where many were more concerned about the sabbath day than about sick people. The "wolves" by which the "lambs" were threatened (v. 3) were not all secular; Jesus and many of his followers suffered most at the hands of religious people.

The seventy were sent out with orders similar to those given earlier to the twelve—that they were not to supply themselves with material things (see 9:3; 10:4). Their lesson was to be that of trust. Later they (at least the twelve) would be told to take along these very possessions (22:35–38). Once one has learned to trust God *for* all, he may then learn to trust him *with* all. The mission was to be one with a message of peace. The commissioned were not to force themselves upon anyone, but were to accept hospitality wherever they were received. They were to eat what was set before them, not raising the question of whether or not food was "clean" (kosher) or "unclean." They were to proclaim the nearness of the kingdom of God. Where they were not received, they were to leave, "shaking the dust from their feet" (v. 11). This was a practice used by Jews when leaving Samaritan or Gentile territory. Thus, Jesus indicated that those who reject the gospel are to be rejected; communication and communion is thus broken.

Jesus took the position that being unclean is not a matter of nationality, race, or ritual, but of failure to submit to the rule (kingdom) of God. The kingdom of God is the sovereign rule, and it is not dependent upon man's response. God is King whatever man does. Those not receiving Christ's messengers were to be warned that the kingdom of God had drawn near in spite of their unbelief. Judgment falls heaviest upon the cities of privilege (vv. 12–16). The greater the opportunity, the greater is the obligation for response—and the penalty for the lack of it.

Jesus saw in the mission of the seventy a decisive victory over Satan. He saw Satan "fall like lightning from heaven" (v. 18, RSV). The kingdom of God was already prevailing over the kingdom of Satan, not in some spectacular world movement, but in the simple preaching and acceptance of the gospel. Jesus rejoiced that the revelation of God was received by "babes" (v. 21). The "wise and understanding" are not excluded unless they put their trust in their own competence. It is through the openness of faith that God is known, not through the competence of the intellect.

III. THE MERCIFUL SAMARITAN (10:25-37)

"Lawyer" is Luke's term for an expert in the Jewish law or a scribe. This lawyer was trying to embarrass Jesus by questioning him in the area of the lawyer's specialty. He asked Jesus what he must do to inherit eternal life. In trying to expose Jesus, he exposed his own inadequate understanding of the intention of the law. Jesus turned the question on the lawyer by asking him what he found in the law. The lawyer quoted Deuteronomy 6:5, the commandment to love God and neighbor with one's whole self. Jesus commended him for answering correctly.

But the scribe was uneasy with this challenging demand; and, wanting to "justify himself," he asked, "And who is my neighbor?" (v. 29). Possibly he wanted to justify himself for asking a question to which he already had the answer, but probably he wanted to justify himself with respect to the command to love his neighbor. The lawyer's very question condemned him. "Who is my neighbor?" is a wrong question because it is a selfish question. The right question would have been, "Am I a neighbor?" The lawyer looked for limits to his obligation to love. To him, his neighbor would be another Pharisee.

Jesus' story of the good Samaritan is among the most beautiful and instructive to be found anywhere. It is significant that Jesus made a Samaritan the hero of the story. Jesus was a Jew, and he told the story to a strict Jew. Jews and Samaritans had been prejudiced and hostile toward one another for centuries. In this story, Jesus depicted a priest and a Levite passing up a man who had been beaten, robbed, and left seriously injured. Indifference alone does not account for their not helping the man. Touching blood or a corpse made one "unclean" as they understood the Jewish Law. By contrast, a Samaritan cared for the victim, giving him first aid and placing him in an inn where he would be cared for. The lawyer had asked, "Who is my neighbor?" Jesus replaced this question with another, "Who of these three seems to you to have become neighbor to the one who fell among thieves?" The Samaritan was a neighbor to the victim of the robbers, because, first of all, he was a neighborly person.

The scribes, or lawyers, knew that love is the primary way, but Jesus showed how love is to come to expression in life. The scribes lacked proper understanding of what love is. This lawyer looked for limits beyond which love was no longer obligated. True love never asks release from obligation. It does not seek the selfish satisfaction of being able to say, "I have gone as far as required and done as much as I am obliged to do." Rather, true love seeks always to satisfy the needs of others. It never feels that it has earned the right to release, reward, or praise (17:10).

Long ago it was pointed out that three approaches to life are illustrated in this story. The robber said, "What is yours is mine, and I will take it." The priest and Levite said, "What is mine is mine, and I will keep it." The Samaritan said, "What is mine is yours, and I will give it." True life belongs to the one who finds the center of his concern outside himself.

Yet another approach to understanding the parable may give deeper insight. With whom do we identify in the story? We would like to place ourselves alongside the "good Samaritan." That role is most attractive, and it is clearly the role that Jesus would have us to assume. But isn't it possible that there is a prior identity that we must see before we can become "good Samaritans"? Must we not first identify with the victim? Must we not first see ourselves in the place of the man in need of compassion and help? Must we not first see ourselves naked, broken, and helpless, forced to accept mercy from an unexpected and undesired source? Only as we thus accept mercy can we begin to understand what mercy is. The victim found out who his neighbor was. One can become the compassionate neighbor only as he first learns to receive mercy.

IV. The Better Part (10:36–42)

The story about Mary and Martha serves to fill out the meaning of the story of the merciful Samaritan. Martha complained to Jesus because Mary sat listening to Jesus while Martha prepared the meal. The great truth in the story of the Samaritan is distorted if one concludes that all he needs to do is to assist people in physical or material need. Practical service is not a substitute for contemplation. Martha's serving of the meal is good, but so is Mary's attention to the words of Jesus. The comparison between the good Samaritan and Martha should not be pressed, for the differences are great. At best, Martha's interests were mixed. Her thoughts were upon her own rights as she understood them as well as for the needs of Jesus.

Verse 42 is of uncertain meaning, for it appears in at least four different forms in various manuscripts of the New Testament. Probably the best reading is the one which closes with "one thing is needful." This could mean that a simple meal would be sufficient rather than the elaborate one about which Martha was distracted. The application, however, is to Mary's choice of that which would never be taken from her. Food satisfies for a time; Christ's word satisfies forever.

V. Jesus' Teaching About Prayer (11:1–13)

Jesus' disciples asked him to teach them to pray. Jesus gave them a model prayer which indicates the proper mood or attitude in prayer and the proper content of prayer. Then, in the story of friends' calling upon one another at midnight, Jesus encouraged one to pray. At the same time, he implied that one does not need to be taught to pray when he knows his need and knows a friend whom he trusts. What does one do when he finds himself without food for his guest who arrives at midnight? If he has another friend whom he really trusts, he knows what to do. He takes his problem to his trusted friend, whatever the inconvenience may be. If one knows his own need and really believes in God, he will pray. One may be taught *how* to pray, but he learns *to pray* out of his sense of dependence upon God.

Prayer is openness to God: asking, seeking, knocking (v. 9). The teaching here is not that selfish requests will be granted. The meaning is that there will be receiving, finding, the opening of doors for the one who asks, seeks, and knocks. What one receives, finds, and has opened to him may be entrusted to God. As an earthly father does not give a snake to the child who asks for a fish, so the Heavenly Father may be trusted to give what is suited to one's needs. His highest gift is the Holy Spirit (v. 13). Our part is to be open to God; his part is to give as he alone knows to give.

The model prayer is simpler in Luke (11:2-4) than in Matthew (6:9-13). The form in Luke is probably earlier. Jesus knew God as Father and wanted his disciples to know him the same way. A Jew used the simple term "father" for his parent, but this term would be unusual in reference to God. In addressing God, he would use a phrase like "our Father" or "God" (Luke 18:13). Luke recorded the single word for "father"—*Abba*—the intimate Aramaic term usually reserved by Jews for one's earthly father. He taught his disciples to address God with this intimate term. But this intimacy was not degrading. He also taught his disciples to hallow God's name. The "name" of God stood for his character as revealed in history and experience. Thus, Jesus combined intimate trust and reverence. The prayer includes concern for the coming of God's kingdom—that his sovereign rule be made real on earth.

Prayer for one's own needs is proper, if properly offered. Man does not live by bread alone (4:4), but neither can he live without it. It is proper to pray for what one needs. Being forgivable is related to being forgiving (v. 4). Unwillingness to forgive betrays the very spirit which shuts one off from forgiveness. If a door is blocked, it prevents passage from either direction. It is not that God is unwilling to forgive anyone, but forgiveness cannot be received by one who is unwilling to give it. Jesus stated, "not the ground on which God bestows forgiveness but the ground on which man can receive it" (Manson).

Temptations and trials were real for Jesus, and he would have his disciples alerted to the threat of them. Verse 4 does not imply that God is the actual source of temptation (see James 1:13). The prayer is stated negatively and positively for emphasis, "Give us not temptation but deliverance."

VI. Signs and Rejection (11:14-36)

This section is held together by the theme of revelation and rejection. Some called Jesus' work of healing a deaf man the work of Beelzebub or Satan (11:14-23) and simply closed their eyes to evidence before them. The crowds clamored for a sign, although they had been given more evidence than they had eyes for (11:29-32). Lamps are lighted that men may see, yet many remain in darkness because their eyes are diseased (11:33-36). Although they beg for more light, their real need is more sight. Those who close their eyes remain in darkness, however great the light about them. This is the thrust of this section: God's giving and man's rejecting; the coming of the kingdom of God and man's resistance to it; God's evident presence, yet man's demand for more evidence.

1. *Beelzebub or the Reign of God?* (11:14–23)

Jesus was accused of casting out demons "by Beelzebub," [1] the prince of demons or Satan (v. 18). Jesus branded this as a senseless charge. Why would Satan destroy his own house? He would not release his own captives. It was Satan's rule (kingdom) which was being overcome. If, on the other hand, what was done was by "the finger of God," [2] this could only mean that the kingdom of God had arrived (v. 20). This affirms that the reign of God is a present reality. It also indicts those who looked upon God's work and called it Satan's work. Only wilful blindness could account for this inexcusable sin. In Jesus Christ the rule of God has come, and there is no place for neutrality; one who is not with him is against him (v. 23).

2. *No Vacuum* (11:24–26)

A house, though swept and put in order, will not remain empty. The forces of evil can be driven out and kept out of one's life only by the power of God. Mere religious reform without the rule of God in a life only opens the way for new "gods" to move in. The Exile cured the Jews of idolatry, but legalism and ritualism came in as more subtle and more dangerous gods.

3. *Jesus' True Kin* (11:27–28)

A woman was impressed with the good fortune of Jesus' mother in having him as her son. Jesus declared instead

---

[1] The spelling and meaning of this name are uncertain; for the manuscripts are divided and the derivations uncertain. Baalzebub means "Lord of flies." (See 2 Kings 1:2ff.) This was possibly a contemptuous change from Baalzebul, "lord of the temple." Beelzebol means "lord of dung."

[2] The "finger of God" is an Old Testament expression, used of God's work in creation (Psalm 8:3), delivering the Israelites from Egypt (Ex. 8:19), and giving the Law (Deut. 9:10). Comparison with parallel passages shows it means "Holy Spirit."

that those are blessed who "hear and observe the word of God." Jesus' true kin are those of faith, not of flesh. Also, they are blessed who hear and obey God's word, not those who only study it.

4. *The Sign of Jonah* (11:29–32)

An evil generation clamored for messianic signs and compelling proofs that the Messiah had come. Jesus offered no new sign to those whose problem was bad eyesight, rather than poor light. He offered them the sign of Jonah and that of the queen of the south (the queen of Sheba). The Ninevites heard only the reluctant preaching of Jonah, yet they repented. The queen of Sheba doubted the stories about Solomon's wisdom and splendor; but when she saw the evidence, she had the honesty to admit that she had been wrong (see 1 Kings 10:1–2). Jesus' generation was confronted by something greater than Jonah or Solomon—the demand of God was present in Christ. Yet they asked for signs! In effect, that generation asked for light when there was abundance of light. They were unable to recognize the light when it shone right on them. They were a people who needed more insight, not more light.

5. *Why a Lamp is Lighted* (11:33–36)

No one lights a lamp to hide it. Jesus did not say that men should not do this; he said that they did not. Neither does God give light in order to hide it. He gives light that we may both receive it and share it. Again, Jesus stressed the problem of poor eyes. If one's eyes are defective, he remains in darkness, however great the light. Repetition of this point was not redundancy in the teaching of Jesus. He encountered no greater problem than the wilful blindness of men. The sin of wilful blindness, shutting one's eyes in the presence of God's light of revelation and redemption, is unpardonable and self-destructive.

VII. PHARISAISM EXPOSED (11:37–54)

The woes pronounced upon the Pharisees have sounded so harsh that many scholars have traced them to the later church in its conflicts with Judaism rather than to Jesus himself. Such a view not only rejects the record offered by Luke and Matthew (23:1–36), but probably misreads it. These "woes" do not represent hatred or animosity nor even negative or destructive satire. Although the words contain a satirical note, they also have a remedial note. Jesus was not an "outsider," heaping scorn upon the Jews. He was a Jew, and he did not purpose to cut himself off from the Jews. He had accepted a Pharisee's invitation to dinner and there spoke upon an issue introduced by his host (v. 38). Jesus' harshest judgments upon Pharisaism were spoken to the Pharisees themselves. These were not hate-filled denunciations but the warning which love dares not neglect to give, however painful or hazardous. Jesus was not pronouncing a curse upon the Pharisees as some seem to think; but he was saying something like "alas for you Pharisees" (NEB). It should also be noted that not all Pharisees are presented in a critical light in the New Testament. Gamaliel and Nicodemus, for example, are portrayed as noble men.

The seemingly harsh words of Jesus are also to be understood in the light of his compassion for the common people. The "lawyers," or scribes, imposed their scholarly understandings upon the untutored masses; and to the simple people of the land, these legalistic rules were "heavy burdens" to be borne (v. 46). Furthermore, by stressing many arbitrary and trivial matters at the expense of justice and love (v. 42), they were locking the door to life to both themselves and those who looked to them for guidance (v. 52).

The "woes" pronounced by Jesus fell upon the "piety" and "virtues" of synagogue religion, and they fall upon Christianity whenever it slips into similar confusion about what really matters. The irony is to be seen in the fact that what Jesus denounced was considered by many to be piety, virtue, and orthodoxy. Jesus' host was astonished that Jesus did not go through purification rites before eating. He countered by exposing the religion which "cleanses the outside of the cup and plate" but leaves the inside filthy (v. 39). To Jesus, the real test of cleanness is inward. What is in the mind or heart is most significant. Jesus is concerned about the outward life, but it is significant only as it reflected the inner life.

One indictment of the "lawyers" was that they built tombs to honor the prophets but were not open to the message of the prophets (vv. 45–52). It is easy to revere dead prophets, safely entombed; but it is another thing to hear God's prophets in one's own time. Would Amos, Micah, John the Baptist, or Jesus fare any better were they to come in our time?

Our culture has seen many examples of Christian men who were cast out because of the stand they took on controversial matters related to race, politics, and social life.

7

Costly Discipleship

12:1 to 14:35

Is salvation free? The answer is both yes and no. It is free
in that we cannot buy it, earn it, or deserve it. We can only
receive it in faith as the gift of God's grace. But in another
sense, salvation costs everything. It cost God his Son. It cost
Jesus his life and, for a time, his family. It costs us everything, for unless one is willing to lose all for Christ, he cannot be his disciple (14:26).

I. DISCIPLESHIP—ITS FREEDOM AND ITS PRICE (12:1-34)

Jesus had been rebuking the scribes and the Pharisees.
Evidently a large and partially hostile mob had gathered.
But Jesus was concerned with his disciples. He wanted them
to understand some blessings and requirements of discipleship. We must accept these teachings, too.

1. Freedom from Fear (12:1-7)

There is a fear of brute force: the fear of physical, political,
or other forces by which one may be injured, killed, or denied
employment. There is fear also of criticism, scorn, or rejection. To be a follower of Christ in a hostile world is to be
exposed to danger. It was so when Jesus walked on earth,
and it is so today. There was no hiding place for him, and
there is none for his followers today.

Fear may drive one to hypocrisy, which Jesus termed "the
leaven of the Pharisees" (12:1). This is the fear that prompts

one to seek escape from criticism or persecution by hiding what he is. Confessing one's faith by word and by manner of life is dangerous business, but this is the Christian's business. The disciple must take the risk of open confession, whatever the cost. He is assured that he has only one to fear; and the one to fear is not he who can destroy the body alone, but he who has the authority to cast one into Gehenna.

Gehenna is a term derived from Ge-Hinnom, Valley of Hinnom, lying southwest of Jerusalem. It was a place of fire worship and human sacrifice in the time of Ahaz, king of Judah about 735–715 B.C. Josiah, king of Judah about 640–609 B.C., turned the place into a rubbish pit (2 Kings 23:10). With its continuous fires, it came to symbolize eternal punishment and supplied the term "Gehenna," the abode of the godless. Properly the one to be feared is God, not Satan. God alone has ultimate authority. Yet God exercises his authority in loving care for his creation. A disciple under persecution for his confession may be tempted to think that his death will be as little noticed as that of a sparrow, but this is not true. God is a loving Father who always cares for his people.

Confession of Christ is perilous, but denial is fatal. Christ's confession or denial of man is bound up with man's confession or denial of Christ. This is not arbitrary. It is not a matter of Christ's attitude toward man or of his willingness to confess man. It is man's condition which determines what Christ must confess about him. The words Jesus spoke here (vv. 8–9) were no doubt in contemplation of the trials to which early Christians were put. Some were offered release if they recanted or denied Christ but death if they confessed him.

The meaning of verse 10 is not clear. Possibly Jesus meant that he does not take personal offense at being slighted by men, but one cannot sin against the light given him by the Holy Spirit and get away with it. Jesus does not get offended and retaliate, but for one to deny himself the Holy Spirit whom Christ brings is to cut oneself off from true life.

The promise that the Holy Spirit will give one what he is to say (12:12) has to do with trials before synagogues or rulers, not with a preacher's sermon or a teacher's lesson. This passage does not authorize one to shun education or necessary preparation. Its force is clear. The disciple's business is to confess Christ before men, not to fret beforehand about the peril of confession or about how he may defend himself before any who might bring him to trial.

The basic witness to Christ should be that borne to him by the very way each Christian lives—naturally and normally —at home, in his work, as he shops, and in all the common places of everyday life; but confession of Christ is also to be made through deliberately chosen actions and words— preaching, teaching, evangelism, institutional ministries, and in every way open to individuals or groups. This is the Christian's business, whatever the hazards. It is our business to witness. It is God's business to take care of our ultimate needs.

2. *Freedom from Greed* (12:13–21)

Jesus refused to be a judge or referee, deciding who would get what among quarreling brothers. He warned against covetousness, for life does not consist of an abundance of material things. One may become enslaved to the very things he seeks to possess. This is illustrated in the story of a rich farmer who dreamed of securing his future through building greater barns to store away greater crops. In the midst of his selfish dreaming, God called him a fool; for the very things which he had called his own were now demanding his soul. He had foolishly laid claim to what was not actually his own: "my fruits . . . my barns . . . my goods . . . my soul" (12:17–19). Verse 20 should be translated, "Fool, in this night they are demanding your soul." The very barns and crops which he called his own were coming to collect. They owned him; he had never owned them.

This passage clearly demonstrates that "soul" may refer to selfhood. Soul is not something ethereal or ghostly; a soul is a person. A soul may "eat, drink, and be merry" (v. 19). It is more biblical to say that one *is* a soul than to say he *has* a soul (compare Gen. 2:7). A lost soul is a lost person. A saved soul is a saved person. Jesus came to save persons in their total selfhood: spiritually, morally, ethically, socially, bodily, and emotionally. His concern included all persons, and it includes each person in his many-sidedness and in all his relationships.

3. *Freedom from Anxiety* (12:22–34)

Jesus warned his disciples against anxiety about things like food and clothing. The word employed may refer to distraction—going to pieces over things. Food and clothing are important, but life is more than food and clothing. Anxiety over things is evil, for it betrays lack of faith in God. Anxiety is unnecessary, for God cares for ravens; and he will care for people if they trust him. It is unprofitable, for one cannot by anxiety add to the length of his life. ("Cubit" in 12:25 may refer to length of life rather than height of body.) Since one must be dependent upon God for life itself, he should be able to trust him for the things needful for life. Anxiety over things is pagan (12:30). The disciple is to believe that God knows his needs and to trust his loving care. His concern is to be for God's kingdom—to live under God's sovereign rule, and to point others to that same rule. Jesus does not promise selfish people all they want; he assures those who submit to God's kingdom rule that they will have all they need.

An amazing truth emerges in the promise, "Fear not, little flock; it is your Father's good pleasure to give you the kingdom" (12:32). To come under God's kingdom rule is to enter into it. Paradoxically, it is when man surrenders to God all claims to sovereignty that he is admitted into God's reign. If one tries to be his own god, he knows only bondage, emptiness, and death. When one yields to God as his sovereign Lord, he finds freedom and life. Treasures on earth are insecure and perishable. There are values which are never lost. One is foolish to bury his heart in what perishes when he may give it to God and to the values which are forever.

II. RESPONSIBLE DISCIPLESHIP (12:35 to 13:17)

1. *The Wise Steward* (12:35–48)

Jesus continued in his effort to teach his disciples. The time of the Lord's return will not be known in advance. What should his disciples be doing meanwhile? The answer is clear: wait, watch, be ready, work, and live responsibly. Jesus taught his disciples to live in the expectancy that both judgment and salvation would be brought to completion when history reaches its goal. His *parousia* (return to earth) would usher history into its final stage. Immediate decisions have eternal consequences. Responsibility is measured by opportunity. The more one is given, the more is required of him. The saying about being "beaten with many stripes" or "beaten with few stripes" (12:47–48) is a way of saying that judgment falls more heavily on some than upon others, determined by one's degree of privilege or opportunity.

2. *Christ's Baptism and Ours* (12:49–53)

Jesus faced an ordeal, and he termed it a "baptism" with which he was to be "baptized" (v. 50). He was not referring to literal baptism in water, for he had been baptized already in that sense. He was speaking of the conflict with his people, their rejection of him, and his approaching death. Jesus came to bring peace on earth (2:14), but the actual result was the "fire" of conflict, division, rejection, and death. He suffered also the pain of separation from his own mother, his brothers, his neighbors at Nazareth, and, finally, his nation as a whole. His mission cost him this separation from those near and dear to him. His mission cost death at the hands of his own people. Likewise, his disciples may know the pain of division so deep as to break the most cherished family ties.

3. *Signs of the Times* (12:54–59)

Men know how to anticipate weather changes by reading the signs of nature. They may be blind to more significant signs. This paragraph is not teaching that men may know in advance the time of the *parousia*. Jesus had just warned that the Son of man would come at an unexpected hour (12:40; compare Matt. 24:36). The reference here is probably to the catastrophe which was about to overtake the Jewish nation and which did take place in A.D. 70 when the Romans destroyed Jerusalem. Jesus did not defend Rome's subjugation of the Jews, but he did warn his people that their salvation would not come through the Zealot uprisings which many called messianic. Jesus urged his people to turn from this suicidal "collision course" with Rome and to turn to the true hope which he offered them as subjects of God's kingdom. (See Luke 21.)

4. *Except Ye Repent* (13:1–9)

These verses provide the only information we have about the Galileans slaughtered by Pilate as they were offering their sacrifices and about the eighteen upon whom the tower of Siloam fell. Pilate, made procurator of Judea in A.D. 26, was capable of such an act as the slaughter of these Galileans. Why the slaying of the Galileans was reported to Jesus is not made clear. Possibly it was believed that to suffer violent death was an indication of divine punishment. Jesus rejected such theology as false. Disaster serves better as an occasion for seeing one's own sin than for judging another. At this very time, Jesus was "journeying toward Jerusalem," seeking to turn his nation from self-destruction to God.

Jesus gave the parable of the fig tree as a further warning to Israel. The fig tree was a symbol of Israel (Hos. 9:10), and probably Jesus saw his journey to Jerusalem as a final attempt to bring Israel to repentance.

5. *A Sabbath Duty* (13:10–17)

Jesus defended his healing of a woman on the sabbath as something that ought to have been done (13:16). An indignant synagogue ruler condemned Jesus for his sabbath healing of a woman who for eighteen years had been unable to stand erect. Jesus was concerned for the woman, not for sabbath rules. He chided those who found no problem in taking care of their animals on the sabbath, but who were indifferent to this woman's need. Jesus' concern for persons above religious forms widened the gap between himself and the synagogue rulers.[1] This is the only recorded occurrence in the later ministry of Jesus of his teaching in a synagogue.

One of the special interests in the Gospel of Luke is that of women. Luke shows the liberation and dignity which Jesus won for women. There is a possible parable in the "loosing" of one who for eighteen years had been "bowed together," or "bent double." Jesus came into a world in which women were denied basic freedom and dignity. Jesus freed women from such status, made them stand erect.

III. THE KINGDOM OF GOD DESCRIBED (13:18–35)

1. *Parables of Mustard Seed and Leaven* (13:18–21)

The kingdom of God is his kingly rule. The kingdom is not the church universal. The church is the community

---

[1] The ruler or leader of a synagogue was responsible for making the arrangements for the synagogue services. He was neither pastor nor preacher for a congregation.

formed under the kingdom or rule of God. Thus church and kingdom are related but not identical.

The kingdom of God has aspects or relations which may be illustrated by parables like those of the mustard seed and the leaven. The parable of the mustard seed illustrates the phenomenal growth of the kingdom; the extension of its rule over the earth, evidenced by the spread of the church on earth. The smallness of mustard seed was proverbial. From such a tiny seed grew a plant ten or twelve feet high. The kingdom of God came in a tiny baby and confronted the world in a man from Nazareth. The power of the kingdom is far greater than was apparent in the seemingly insignificant appearance of Jesus of Nazareth.

The parable of the leaven probably illustrates the dynamic and invincible nature of the kingdom. It comes in Jesus Christ as a personal and transforming presence. It works like leaven works, inwardly and silently, yet with transforming power.

2. *Those Feasting in the Kingdom of God* (13:22–30)

The question about whether few or many would be saved was often debated by the rabbis. A Jewish apocryphal writing held that many have been created but few would be saved (2 Esdras 8:1–3). Although salvation begins within the here and now, it is salvation in the future world which is under consideration here.

Jesus did not answer the question as it was put to him, as though a fixed number were elected to salvation, whether few or many. Rather he cautioned his questioners that for them there was a more important question than the speculative one about the number of the saved: Would they be included? He warned that neglect "to enter in through the narrow door" could be fatal, for the time would come when the "door" would be shut. No belated weeping and wailing would avail.

Furthermore, his hearers were not to presume upon the matter of their national identity. From east and west and north and south people would come to share with patriarchs and prophets in the messianic feast of the kingdom of God. And this feast would be closed to many Jews who had excluded themselves by unbelief. Jesus explained that some who think themselves to be first will be last, and some who think themselves to be last will be first. Salvation is not hereditary or by national or racial identity. It depends upon entering through the narrow door of faith into the kingdom of God—coming under his kingly rule.

3. Jerusalem Loved and Lost (13:31–35)

It is not clear whether the Pharisees who warned Jesus about the intention of Herod Antipas to kill him were friends or foes. In any event, Jesus refused to be intimidated. Calling Herod "that fox" reflects Jesus' knowledge of and judgment upon Herod's evil ways. Although Herod ruled over Galilee, Jesus was determined to remain in Galilee until he had completed his work there. From Galilee he would go on to Jerusalem where the danger would be even greater. Herod could not dictate the way Jesus went about accomplishing his purposes.

Jesus felt that he must go to Jerusalem, even though he anticipated rejection there. His cry over Jerusalem reflects his deep love for that city and supports the record of John's Gospel to the effect that he visited it a number of times. Luke told of only one visit to Jerusalem by Jesus, that which resulted in his death. However, from 9:51 on, Jerusalem is kept before Luke's readers. Jesus' cry over Jerusalem is clear as to its many implications: "I would . . . but ye would not" (13:34). Salvation may be offered but not imposed. Fates are not fixed by divine decree but by man's response to God's offer. In A.D. 70, Jerusalem was left in ashes, a part of the "desolation" from which Jesus sought to save her.

VI. WARNINGS GIVEN IN A PHARISEE'S HOUSE (14:1–24)

1. *The Worth of a Man* (14:1–6)

Jesus exposed the hardheartedness of religious leaders who prized sabbath observance above caring for the needs of people. Jesus went to eat with Pharisees as well as with "publicans and sinners." On this occasion, Jesus was in the home of a Pharisee on the sabbath. The Pharisees were watching to see if he would observe their sabbath regulations. Except where life was in danger, they forbade care for the sick. But Jesus healed the sick man and brought the Pharisees under judgment from their own laws. They would rescue an animal that had fallen into a well on the sabbath. If one's animal could be rescued on the sabbath, why not heal a man on the sabbath? Which is worth more, a beast or a man? Which is worth more, a man or the sabbath rules?

2. *A Lesson in Humility* (14:7–11)

Jesus observed guests who were seeking the chief couches at the banquet. The host had authority to assign to each guest his place. Jesus warned that one could be humiliated by being demoted to a place of less honor, whereas honor could come to one who was called to a higher place after he had taken a lower one. Jesus was not teaching the "pride that apes humility." Simply to take a lower place with a view to promotion would be another form of selfish pride. True exaltation belongs to those who do not only take the lower place, but who are willing to occupy it. Verse 11 is the key verse, and it states a basic truth in paradoxical form: "Everyone who exalts himself shall be humbled, and everyone who humbles himself shall be exalted."

3. *Hosting the Have Nots* (14:12–14)

Hospitality, if Christian, is not for hire. To invite another with a view to gaining an invitation from him is a selfish game which any pagan can play. Pagan society is marked by its rounds of social obligations incurred and paid back. Jesus prescribed another pattern in commanding his hearers to invite the "have nots"—those unable to pay back the favor. Such action derives from the divine love which seeks to serve, not the world's so-called love which seeks to use other people. Christian hospitality is to be offered as something freely given, not as a bargaining for something in return. It is to be offered to people who have nothing to give, including people who may not even be "prospects" for one's own church.

4. *The Slighted Invitation* (14:15–24)

Amidst all the scrambling for the chief couches at the world's banquets (14:7) and the social climbing which invites in order to be invited (14:12), there is a strange indifference to the great "supper" to which God invites mankind. Jesus gave the parable of a man who invited guests to a "great supper," only to have them excuse themselves from it because of the purchase of a field or oxen or because of a new wife. Persons who make such excuses deny themselves the privilege of the supper, but the guest room is filled with others. This judgment is pronounced upon the people of privilege. Again we are reminded of the self-imposed rejection of the Jews and the giving of the gospel to the Gentiles, a major theme of Luke-Acts.

Entrance into the kingdom of God is by his invitation. Only because God calls may man answer; yet God's calling is not coercive, for man may refuse to answer. The New Testament knows no doctrine of irresistible grace. Although foolish beyond comprehension, man may and does resist God's grace. Election is not the choice of one instead of another; it is God's choosing man so that man may choose him. Jesus extended the invitation to the "messianic banquet" first to the Jews, many of whom declined to attend.

Luke-Acts shows how the invitation went ultimately to "tax gatherers and sinners" in Israel, and to Samaritans and Gentiles outside Israel. We today may abuse the same privilege and lose it just as did the people of privilege in Jesus' day.

V. COUNTING THE COST OF DISCIPLESHIP (14:25–35)

Jesus wanted followers, but not on just any basis. He was on his way to Jerusalem and the cross, and only the one who bore his own "cross" could truly follow him. The cross stands for death. In principle it is death to self in the act of surrender to Christ. It is the denial of the self that would have its being apart from God and others. Although it is death, it is also life. The cross is life through death. It is finding a new way of life in rejecting the way of self-love, self-trust, and self-assertion.[2]

What Jesus said about hating one's own father and mother, wife and children, brothers and sisters, and his own life also is neither to be explained away nor taken out of context. The words sound extremely harsh. This form of speech is known as an *oxymoron*, that is, a deliberately harsh statement. It is precisely because family ties are precious that willingness to lose them is a sacrifice. It would have been pointless had Jesus said, "Except you hate mosquitoes you cannot be my disciple." These words were spoken to multitudes who thought that they wanted to follow Jesus. Many came to him with shallow understanding and with selfish or unworthy motives. Jesus' mission cost him his family, for a time at least; it cost him the good will of his home community and nation; and it cost him his life. Any who would follow him must be willing to lose all as the cost of discipleship.

The parables of the builder of a tower and the king going

---

[2] See Stagg, *New Testament Theology*, Nashville: Broadman Press, 1962, pp. 122-148 for an extensive discussion of the meaning of Jesus' death.

to war (14:28–31) stress the importance of counting the cost of an undertaking before committing oneself to it. Jesus is not saying that it is better not to begin than to fail. His point is that one should count the cost before beginning. Acceptance of Christ is costly; so is rejection. One ought to count the cost of following and also of not following. It is the former which is stressed in this context.

True discipleship is as costly today as when Luke wrote. The world does not change except superficially. It has new gadgets but the same fears, hatreds, prejudices, lusts, greed, and cruelty. If the church is at peace with the world, it is the "church" which has changed, not the world. True Christianity is always a judgment upon the ways and values of the world, and the world resents and resists judgment. Being true to Christ today may cost one his job or his life. It may cost a pastor his pulpit or a layman a position or a promotion. It may cost a statesman an election or a young person social acceptance. Discipleship is costly; not to follow the Christ is even costlier.

8

God's Joy

15:1 to 19:27

"BLOOD IS THICKER than water" is an old proverb referring to the strong ties which bind families together. Persons who have known the joy of strong family bonds are in a favorable position to understand God's joy in recovering his people and their joy in being restored to God's family. This is what the gospel is about. It is the story of God's sorrow and God's joy. It is the story of broken and restored relationships.

Much of the section before us (15:1 to 19:27) seems to have little to do with joy, for it takes us right up to Jerusalem where Jesus was crucified. God's joy of saving those who repent and God's sorrow of losing those who refuse his love are experienced together in the work of redemption. The writer of Hebrews captured this blending of elements when he pictured Jesus as one "who for the joy that was set before him endured the cross, despising the shame . . ." (Heb. 12:2). This is the story Luke's Gospel tells.

I. GOD'S JOY IN RECOVERING THE LOST (15:1–32)

Verses 1–2 give the setting for the understanding of the three parables which follow. To ignore the setting is to miss the meaning in the parables. Especially misleading is the common practice of isolating "the parable of the prodigal son" from its setting and from the larger story which includes "the elder brother."

The Pharisees and scribes criticized Jesus because he received sinners and ate with them. Jesus answered their criticism with three parables. If the Pharisees and scribes had known God's sorrow in the loss of even one person and his joy over one sinner's repentance, they would not have censured Jesus for eating with publicans and sinners.

The three parables are commonly called the parables of the lost sheep, the lost coin, and the prodigal son. This labeling misses the emphasis of Jesus. They are actually the parables of the good shepherd, the diligent woman, and the loving father. *In each story the emphasis falls upon the joy of recovering what was lost.* The third parable is the climactic one, and it most fully answers the murmuring of the Pharisees against Jesus.

1. *The Joy of the Shepherd* (15:3–7)

Ninety-nine sheep safely in the fold did not lessen the shepherd's concern for the one that was missing. Love knows the value of one. In its strange arithmetic, love is not diminished by being given. A parent does not love one child less because he also loves, and is concerned about, his other children. The concerned shepherd sought the lost sheep until he found it, took it home, and called in the neighbors to rejoice with him. The statement that God rejoices more over one sinner who repents than over ninety-nine "righteous persons who need no repentance" is not to be taken out of context. God is pleased with obedience, but not with proud self-righteousness. Repentant sinners gave Jesus more joy than the proud Pharisees who thought they needed no repentance. The Pharisees needed to learn that one cannot understand what God's righteousness is until he first knows himself to be broken and lost.

2. *The Joy of the Diligent Woman* (15:8–10)

The lessons here parallel those of the story above: the value of one, the search for the lost, the joy of recovery. A woman who lost and then found a coin called in her friends and neighbors to share her joy. Even so, God rejoices over one sinner who repents. Those who murmured against Jesus did not understand that God does not easily let go of sinful man. That is our hope. Recovering the lost is God's joy.

3. *The Joy of the Loving Father* (15:11–32)

Jesus said, "A certain man had two sons. . . ." He did not say, "There was a prodigal son. . . ." In the story, a father had two sons who were lost to him. The younger was recovered; the older one gave no sign of becoming a real son. The younger son was mixed up about life, but at last he found it precisely where he had missed it. The older son never left home and yet never knew what it was to be truly a son or a brother. The "prodigal son" typifies the "publicans and sinners" whom Jesus received and with whom he ate. The "elder brother" typifies the self-righteous Pharisees and scribes who murmured against Jesus because he received sinners and ate with them. The father of the two sons typifies God who yearns for the recovery of publicans and Pharisees, "sinners" and scribes.

The younger son demanded his part of the family estate, left home, and tried to find a happy life in a "far country." The father divided up "the living" (*bios*), but this did not provide the son with life (*zoē*). Life is more than things. Love and life cannot be imposed upon a son, not even by a loving father. The younger son learned the hard, painful way that life cannot be gained by leaving home or be bought at the world's markets. He finally "came to himself," seeing the nothingness of his existence. It was the remembrance of a loving father which turned him homeward. Earlier he was unwilling to be called a son; now he felt unworthy to be so called. Earlier he had demanded his rights; now he submitted to the claims and the care of the father. On his part, the loving father awaited only the son's willingness to receive. The father gave more than the son asked. He received him not as a hired servant but as a son. The father gave him not only clothing and a banquet, but first of all himself.

The "elder brother" rejected his brother and his father. He boasted of "slaving" through many years for his father and complained of not being paid. He had the heart of a slave, not of a son. He was lost to home even though he never left it. His kinship was of the flesh but not of spirit. The elder brother rebuked his father for receiving back the prodigal, just as the Pharisees rebuked Jesus for eating with sinners. The elder brother failed to understand the father's joy, just as the Pharisees failed to understand God's joy in recovering lost sinners.

The parable is chiefly about the father. God is like the father who grieves over the loss of both sons. God is like the seeking father, the waiting father, the father who cannot contain his joy when the prodigal returns home. God is like the father who pleaded with the elder son to become a part of a restored family. God loves publicans and Pharisees. His love can only be offered; it cannot be imposed. His sorrow is in his rejected love; his joy is in one's willingness to be accepted. In the presence of a loving father, the prodigal was willing to accept the father's acceptance of him, even though he knew that in his own rights he was unacceptable. This is the glorious gospel: God's willingness to accept the unacceptable! This is our calling—to accept God's acceptance of us, knowing that as sinners we are really not acceptable. In this is God's joy and our joy.

Luke 15 tells of God's joy in receiving sinners. It also tells of the unwillingness of some religious people—the Pharisees —to accept people whom Jesus accepted. Do we today accept all whom Christ accepts? Jesus never gives the option of receiving him apart from receiving his people. To accept him requires that we accept them. To reject them is to reject him.

II. Joy Lost in the Tyranny of Money (16:1–31)

1. *The Shrewd Steward* (16:1–13)

Money usually proves to be a tyrant over man: "The love of money is a root of all kinds of evil" (1 Tim. 6:10). But money is not evil in itself. It can be made to serve what is good. Possibly the lesson in 16:9, "Make for yourselves friends out of the mammon of unrighteousness," is that money can serve to unite people, although normally it divides them. Whenever one sees himself as owner, saying, "This is mine," material things can only divide. If I say, "This is mine," I also imply, "It is not yours, and it is not God's." If I see myself as a steward, then I acknowledge that all belongs to God and that it is entrusted to me in the service of others. Thus, in the "stewardship" approach to money or property, one is united to God and man. In the "owner" approach, he is estranged from God and man. In the parable of the unjust steward (16:1–9), we are taught to put money to its proper service, that of friendship or community rather than enmity and division.

The parable of the unjust steward might be called that of the shrewd steward. (A steward was a business manager.) The only thing he was commended for was his shrewdness. He had mismanaged his master's estate, and he was ordered to turn in his books. While he yet held the office, with "power of attorney," or legal power, to transact business for his master, he moved quickly to ingratiate himself with others to whom he would look for favors after the loss of his job. He allowed them to pay off their debts at a discount. Before his time ran out, he acted to insure his own financial future. Jesus urged his disciples to make the most of opportunity as they had it. What one does with present opportunity affects him in this life and the next. Furthermore, one's true relationship to God and man may be reflected in matters of material things.

Man may serve God or mammon, but he cannot belong to both. Only by yielding to the sovereignty of God may one be delivered from the tyranny of materialism. There is no better place in which to find one's true God and one's true joy than in looking to God for deliverance from the love of money that is the root of all kinds of evil.

2. Fooling Self but Not God (16:14-31)

Three seemingly unrelated subjects are held together as Jesus' answer to the disposition of the Pharisees to justify themselves (16:15). They scoffed at what Jesus taught about money, they themselves being "lovers of money" (16:14). Jesus warned them that, though they "justified themselves," God knew their hearts as they were. He gave three illustrations of God's overruling of man's self-justification: (1) in man's attempt to force God's kingdom (16:16-17); (2) in divorce (16:18); and (3) in the story of the rich man and Lazarus (16:19-31).

Jesus saw that some were trying to force the kingdom of God, or use it for their own purposes. These were people like the Zealots who did not submit to God's rule, but rather tried to force God to carry out their political ambitions with respect to their nation. Another illustration of man's futile attempt to justify himself related to divorce. Many of the Pharisees taught that a man might divorce his wife for any reason—for a poorly prepared meal or because he had found a more attractive woman. They called this divorce, but God called it adultery (16:18).

The story of the rich man and Lazarus provides a further illustration of man's futile attempt to justify himself. The rich man lived in luxury while Lazarus lay sick and hungry at his gate. In Hades, the rich man was the same self-centered man, complaining about his personal lack and crying out for attention and help. He was an egocentric person in Hades, as he had been before his death. Even his plea that his five brothers be warned against a like fate was only a thinly-veiled effort to justify himself. In effect he was saying, "If I had been adequately warned, I would not have ended up this way." Abraham corrected him, saying that the problem was not that the warnings were insufficient, but that they were unheeded: "If Moses and the prophets they hear not, neither if one arise from the dead will they trust" (16:31). The rich man and his five brothers needed better ears, not a clearer warning. The rich man was to blame for his plight, yet he tried to justify himself. He only fooled himself, not God.

The chief lesson of this story may be that one's true attitude and relationship with God are reflected in his attitude toward his fellowman. One cannot divorce his relationship with man from that with God. While they are not the major thrust of this passage, some additional truths can be gleaned from Jesus' teachings here. There is the fact of life beyond death. It is implied that the future life is bodily, not ghostly, and that one goes immediately into God's presence (while others are yet in this life). There is life beyond physical death. We will recognize one another as individual persons, and one's destiny is determined in this life.

III. FORGIVENESS, FAITH, DUTY, AND GRATITUDE (17:1–19)

Serving God through serving others can be a joy or a burden. Attitude makes the difference. Two examples of persons are given for sharp contrast; the self-centered rich man who found himself separated from God and God's people by a "great fixed gulf" (Luke 16), and the disciple who helps those who stumble. The latter is the person who has the kind of faith which undertakes to "move mountains," sees his best service as nothing more than what he owes God, and who has a deep sense of gratitude for blessings received. These are the marks of discipleship which Luke brings together in these nineteen verses.

Jesus taught that it would be better for one to be drowned in the sea than to cause a "little one" to stumble (17:1–2). A little one may be a child or any childlike or trusting person. It is better to be dead than to cause another's downfall. But it is not enough simply to play a negative role in not causing others to stumble. The follower of Jesus has a positive role when he sees another fall. It is to help him up. If one sins and repents seven times a day, he is to be forgiven. This is a major way in which one may lift the person who has stumbled (17:3–4).

When the apostles asked Jesus to increase their faith, he stressed the nature of faith rather than its quantity. Christian faith is trust, openness to God, and commitment to him. To have his kind of faith at all is to open up infinite possibilities for life. Faith is not a magic charm for removing literal mountains, but faith is a channel through which may flow God's infinite power. In effect, Jesus told the apostles that the way to have their faith increased was to act in terms of the faith they already had (17:5–6).

An old proverb says that a mother's work is never done; neither is the work of a servant of Christ. A Christian can never "pay his debt" to God. When he has done his best, he can only say: "I have done what I ought to have done." This is not a complaint; this is joy. The "elder brother" was miserable in his complaint that he was not rewarded for his work (15:29), and the rich man was miserable as he had thought only for himself (16:19–31). But the servant who acknowledges his indebtedness to God finds joy in serving, regretting only that he cannot offer more.

Gratitude is another ingredient in joy, and it belongs

properly to discipleship. Ten lepers were cleansed; but only one, a Samaritan, returned to give thanks (17:11–19). Luke's concern with a gospel for all people is served in this story. The incident illustrates the concern Jesus had for people beyond Israel and the grateful response to him by people outside Judaism. The response of this "stranger" foreshadowed the outreach of the gospel to all the world.

IV. The Certainty of God's Kingdom (17:20 to 18:8)

God's kingdom is his sovereign rule. This means that God is King. God will not abdicate his throne, and no power can dethrone him. In his own time and in his own way he will bring both judgment and redemption to their goal. There is no question about the victory of God's kingdom. The one question is, "When the Son of man comes, will he find faith on the earth?" (18:8).

The Pharisees demanded of Jesus when the kingdom of God would come (17:20). To them the kingdom of God would mean the liberation of Israel from Rome's rule, the punishment of the wicked heathen, and the vindication of Israel. To them the coming of God's kingdom would be outward and catastrophic, like the overthrow of one nation by another. Jesus warned that the kingdom of God would not come like that, as something which could be observed outwardly. It comes within a person as one yields to Christ, the one whom God has anointed to reign.

Jesus anticipated that his disciples would share some of the Pharisees' misunderstanding of the kingdom. Days would come when they, too, would wonder why God did not act in judgment against the wicked and in vindication of his people (17:22). People of every age have wondered why God does not act more decisively and outwardly with respect to good and evil. Why do the wicked seem to prosper and the righteous to suffer? Often it seems that good people suffer poverty, sickness, and oppression while wicked people get rich and powerful and do not even have ulcers as a penalty.

Jesus answered both the Pharisees and his disciples with several assurances. God does know the difference between the righteous and the wicked, and he is not indifferent to the variance. God does act in judgment and in vindication. Both begin in this life, but not necessarily in outwardly observable ways. Both judgment and vindication will be brought to completion in God's own time. Distinctions between God's people and those who are not are based upon God's measurements and not man's. It is not a simple matter of being Jew or Roman. "In the days of the Son of man" (17:26), God's dividing line will run through a family, taking one and rejecting another, even though they be two brothers sleeping in one bed (17:34). The line may run between two women of the same family or neighborhood, taking one and rejecting the other as they grind meal together (17:35). Although it may seem that God either does not care or is unable to bring the wicked to judgment, his judgment is as certain as is the gathering of vultures upon a dead body (17:37).

The parable of a poor widow and a heartless judge offers a lesson by contrast (18:1–8). It may seem that God does nothing to avenge the righteous, but they may be assured that God will act properly. The poor widow's case rested with a wicked judge who neither feared God nor respected man (18:4). For no better reason than to avoid being "pestered to death," he avenged the widow. Does this mean that God is like the heartless judge? Does he operate upon the principle that "the wheel that squeaks gets the grease"? To the contrary, God's people have a surer hope in a righteous God than the widow had in the unrighteous judge. The question is not that implied in the Pharisees' demand or the disciples' doubts. It is not a question of whether God will judge the wicked and avenge the righteous. God's sovereign rule is certain. The question is not about God but about man. Will the Son of man find faith on the earth? God can be trusted! Our part is to trust. If we trust God, we will leave the matter of judgment and vindication in his hands, the logical and safe place.

V. ENTRANCE INTO GOD'S KINGDOM (18:9 to 19:27)

God is ready to admit one into his kingdom, but how does one enter? To put it another way, salvation is a gift ready for receiving; but how does one receive it? The answer has to do with attitude. In various ways, this is spelled out in a long section including 18:9 to 19:27. In brief, God's great gift of salvation can be received only by those who have that openness to God which is called faith or trust. This is a childlike quality. Salvation is not merchandise to be bought at a bargain counter. It is a gift awaiting the one who knows his need and asks. It is God's gift to the one who has the openness to receive it.

A Pharisee and a publican went to the temple to pray (18:9-14). The publican went home "justified," but not the Pharisee. What made the difference? The Pharisee was of that group who "trusted in themselves" and despised others. He confessed other peoples' sins but not his own. In his pride and self-righteousness, he chose to separate himself from other people. Thus, he unintentionally cut himself off from God. He prayed "with himself." Since he confessed no sin, God has no way to forgive him. The publican, by contrast, was so painfully aware of his sin that he could only cry out for mercy, believing that God is merciful. This was the openness through which he received salvation.

Jesus taught that one can receive the kingdom only as a child (18:15-17). It is not the child's innocence but his openness to receive that is the point. It is a child's disposition to trust. He knows his dependence and is not too proud to receive.

A rich ruler came to Jesus for eternal life but left without

it (18:18–30). Why? He came as a bargainer, sincerely
seeking and prepared to pay; but as a bargainer he was in-
terested only if what he got seemed to be worth more than
the cost. "What must I do to inherit eternal life?" was a
selfish question on his lips. He came to get, but not to submit. Knowing the key to the man's problem, Jesus tested
him at the point of his possessions. Would he give up all
for Jesus? Not as a bargainer! Riches so enslave one that
it is only by a miracle of grace that one who has trusted in
his riches can yield to Christ alone as Master. By Bible mea-
sures, most Americans are rich. Do we make money the
measure of life?

Even Peter had much yet to learn about discipleship (18:
28–34). Peter reminded Jesus of what he and others had
given up to follow him. Jesus gave assurance that any sacrifice
is more than repaid, but discipleship is more than seeking
reward. Rejection and death awaited Jesus at Jerusalem, and
this could be the fate of any follower of his.

The nature of salvation is illustrated in the conversion of
Zacchaeus (19:1–10). Jesus astonished many by accepting
the hospitality of this tax gatherer. Whatever may first have
attracted Zacchaeus to Jesus, curiosity or need, the miracle
of conversion occurred in Jesus' presence. A self-centered,
money-minded man suddenly was concerned to make amends
for wrongs done to other people. This attitude of concern
for others and for right was outward evidence that salvation
had come to Zaccheus. Luke's interest in the gospel for all
people is also served in this story. Jesus sought out a man
despised by the religious authorities. Jesus sought him out
because he was lost, not because he was good. This un-
promising person was seen to be a true "son of Abraham,"
not because he was good or because he was a Jew, but because his life was opened to God and to others—to receive
and to give.

By one sarcastic word Jesus could have exploited the community's prejudices against Zacchaeus, who was an easy target, as he was perched in the tree. Jesus could have won a following at Zacchaeus' expense. Instead, he risked alienation, in fact he did alienate the town, by entering the home of Zacchaeus. Jesus accepted an "unacceptable" man and won him to a new way of life.

The parable of the pounds (19:11–27) illustrates a great principle, "Unto everyone who has shall be given; but from him who has not shall be taken away even that which he has" (19:26). The one who "has it" is the one who has the proper attitude or disposition. The servants who trusted their master, who were concerned for the increase of his holdings, and who ran the risks involved in seeking a gain for their master were the ones who "had it." Their trust in and devotion to their master was what made it possible for him to entrust them with yet more. One servant tried to play safe, thinking that he would best secure his own interests by risking nothing. He had neither trust in nor devotion for his master. Whereas the other servants risked their own security in the effort to serve their master, this selfish and faithless servant sought only to save himself.

It is strange, but true, that one lives by dying, receives by giving, becomes first through willingness to be last, is forgiven by accepting condemnation, and is made secure by willingness to risk all for the Master. This is the joy set before us. It is ours if we have the faith to receive it.

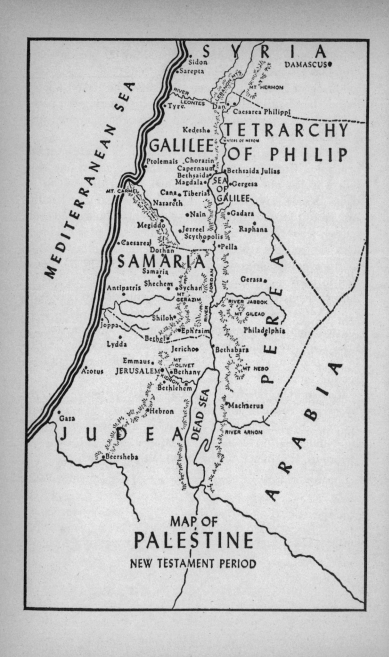

MAP OF
PALESTINE
NEW TESTAMENT PERIOD

Part 5

JESUS' MINISTRY IN JERUSALEM

Luke 19:28 to 24:53

For Jesus all roads led not to Rome, but to Jerusalem. It was at the center of the Jewish world that he and his nation must come to terms with one another. It was there that Jesus must offer himself openly and decisively to his people, forcing them into the agony of decision in which they must decide for or against him. The Saviour of the world would not bypass his own nation. The gospel for all nations was to be preached first to the Jews. Luke's story is not of the rejection of Israel in favor of the world, but of the tragic refusal of Jesus' own dear people to become a part of the larger world in receiving him as Saviour and Lord.

What occurred at Jerusalem is the story of man's worst deed and God's best deed. The two deeds occurred together, but they are not to be confused. God gave life precisely where man took life. There is redemption in what God did, but not in what man did. What God did at Golgotha was a beautiful and redemptive act of reclaiming love. What man did was an ugly and evil act of rejection, betrayal, and murder. God's will was behind Christ's willingness to die, but God's will was not behind man's willingness to kill.[1] Two ways met at Golgotha: God's way of self-giving and man's way of self-assertion. Man's way seemed to prevail as Jesus was put to death, but actually this was the triumph

---

[1] For an extended discussion of the death of Jesus, see Frank Stagg, *New Testament Theology*, pp. 122-148.

of God's way over man's way. Life proved to be stronger than death, both in the resurrection of Jesus and in the transforming of lives from the way that takes life to the way that gives life. That the cross is the wisdom and power of God (1 Cor. 1:18) is demonstrated in every conversion of man from his self-centeredness to the way of the cross.

Luke's Gospel closes at Jerusalem with Jewish Christians worshiping in the Temple. The book of Acts, the second volume of Luke-Acts, closes with Paul preaching an unhindered gospel in Rome—the capital city of the world. What began in Judaism was intended for the world, the gospel for all nations. To turn this around, what by Luke's time had become a world religion is shown in the Gospel of Luke to have begun in the best Jewish piety. The Gospel of Luke begins (2:22) and closes with pictures of the family and the earliest followers of Jesus at worship in the Temple at Jerusalem.

9

Last Ministry in the Temple

19:28 to 21:38

JESUS HAD LONG KNOWN that his date with destiny would be kept at Jerusalem (9:31). Knowing that the days in which he would be "received up" were near, he had "stedfastly set his face to go to Jerusalem" (9:51). Luke kept this fact before his readers (13:22; 17:11; 18:31; 19:28). Jesus not only foresaw but carefully planned a visit to Jerusalem in which he would offer himself to his nation as her Messiah, as King of peace.

I. ROYAL ENTRY INTO JERUSALEM (19:28-46)

Commonly called "the triumphal entry," this is better understood as the royal entry of Jesus into Jerusalem. Jesus carefully chose the manner of his entry so as to declare both the fact and the nature of his messianic claim. He came as a king, but not as a worldly king. He chose to ride a young colt and not a white horse—the symbol of military triumph—for he rejected the role of political Messiah. He had not come to establish a political state, freed from Roman rule. He had come to offer peace, not war (2:14; 19:38). He had come to bring in the kingdom of God, not to restore Israel to a dominant place among the nations of the world. Many looked for a Messiah who would lead armies to defeat Rome and thus bring in God's kingdom. Jesus came to create a new people of God under the kingdom of God. He came not to take the lives of Israel's enemies but to give his own. The

117

weapon of his warfare was not a sword but a cross—his own.

The care with which Jesus planned his royal entry into Jerusalem is reflected even in the arrangements made for the colt. To avoid miscarriage of plans, a password seems to have been selected. Thus, the owners would know to whom to release the colt. It is merely a guess—but not an improbable one—that Lazarus, whose home was at nearby Bethany, may have been the one entrusted to make the arrangements.

The peace Jesus offered Jerusalem was rejected, and unwittingly Jerusalem chose destruction for herself (19:42–44). Jerusalem's sad fate is anticipated in the words, "If you had known in this day, even you, the things which belong to peace, but now they are hidden from your eyes" (v. 42). They were blind to what Jesus tried to show them, because they saw only what they wanted to see—a political Messiah whom they could use for their temporal goals.

The description of Jerusalem under siege and utter destruction (vv. 43–44) foretold the fate which overtook Jerusalem in A.D. 70. At that time Roman armies, after a long siege, broke through the defensive walls and burned the city to the ground—including the Temple. They slaughtered all the people who were not fortunate enough to escape by flight. This fate overtook Jerusalem as she placed all her hopes in a messianic deliverance of a political-military type. It was from this fate that Jesus tried to turn his people, offering them a true kingdom which would never fail.

II. The Authority of Christ (19:47 to 20:18)

1. *Authority Questioned* (20:1–8)

When Jesus cleansed the Temple and taught the people there, it is not surprising that the chief priests, the scribes, and the elders asked him, "By what authority do you these things? or who gave you this authority?" (20:2). These were recognized officials and teachers among the Jews, and Jesus was upsetting many well-established patterns. They had not only the right but the responsibility to ask Jesus for his credentials. Jesus did not question their right to ask about his authority; he challenged their sincerity. They were not honest in their question, and he exposed their hypocrisy. He did it in the most devastating way, by forcing them to condemn themselves.

Jesus questioned his opponents about the baptism of John. Was it of God or of men (20:4)? They huddled to search for an answer and decided to be evasive, pleading that they did not know. John's ministry had been completed and the common people were persuaded that he was a prophet; yet, these religious leaders claimed that they did not know whether John was a true prophet or not. It was not that they did not know or could not know; it was that they were unwilling to know by what authority John or Jesus spoke. Jesus refused to discuss the matter of his authority with hypocrites who rejected the very authority of the God they pretended to honor. The authority of God is acknowledged in obedience to him, not simply in talk about authority.

2. *Wilful Rejection of Authority and Its Crushing Consequences* (20:9–18)

The parable of the vineyard illustrates one major point: To reject God's offer of salvation is to bring utter ruin upon oneself. But a cluster of truths are set forth in the parable, all related to the question of authority raised by the religious rulers.

In the parable, some tenants beat the servants whom the owner sent to collect the rent at harvest time. They even killed the owner's son, hoping to seize the son's inheritance. They did more than reject the servants and the son. They defied the authority of the man who was the owner of the vineyard—the master of the servants and the father of the son. The defiant tenants had seemingly prevailed over the servants and the son, but they yet had to reckon with the owner of the vineyard.

The analogy is obvious. When men reject God's prophets or his Son, they defy God's authority; and they must answer to him. To reject Jesus Christ is to reject the cornerstone to the house God builds. Wilful blindness does not put out the light, but it does put out sight. To pretend to respect God's authority, yet reject it as it comes to us in his Son, Jesus Christ, is to be crushed by the consequences of such stubborn resistance. To stumble over the stone is bad enough, but to persist in wilful disobedience is to have it fall with pulverizing force upon oneself.

Another way of putting the truth of 20:18 is to say that, some way or other, man must be broken and die. This death must be either in salvation or in judgment. One must yield to Christ as saving Lord or as final judge.

III. ATTEMPTS TO TRAP JESUS (20:19–44)

1. *Tribute to Caesar* (20:19–26)

The scribes and chief priests, already determined to have Jesus killed, sought to trap him in a dilemma. They sent spies to him with a trick question, "Is it lawful to pay tribute to Caesar, or not?" (20:22).

Tribute was money levied by the Roman Government upon a captive nation. To pay it was both an economic burden and a humiliation, for it was tangible acknowledgment of servitude. The Zealots among the Jews were the extreme "right wing" party of nationalists who considered it a betrayal of their nation thus to serve Rome. The Sadducees were at the opposite extreme. As the priestly collaborators with Rome, they gained powerful and lucrative positions through their subservience. They supported the payment of the tribute to Rome. Of course, the Romans themselves would consider it treason to refuse to pay the tax.

The test question seemed to force Jesus into a dilemma. To say that the tribute should be paid would be to offend the Zealots. To say that the tribute should not be paid would be to play into the hands of the Romans. Jesus did not evade the question; neither did he fall into the trap. Rather, he turned the dilemma upon those who asked the question. Calling for a coin, he asked whose picture and inscription was upon it. The answer was inescapable, "Caesar's." Jesus made a far-reaching pronouncement: "Give back to Caesar what belongs to Caesar and to God what belongs to God" (20:25). The very fact that they had Caesar's coin showed that they themselves had acknowledged the Roman state. Because they had accepted the state's benefactions, they were already in debt to the state; so it had claims upon them.

Jesus, in this teaching, recognized the validity of civil government. Without condoning any particular form of government or any particular public official, Jesus did endorse the principle of government—an ordered society rather than anarchy. But Jesus did not teach that "Caesar," or state, is sovereign over one realm and God over another. God does not divide his rule with "Caesar." The state has no authority independent of God. The state itself is answerable to God, who alone has absolute and ultimate authority over all that is. Whenever a state or any institution of the world claims to be totalitarian, it is idolatrous—a false god. The state has valid claims upon us, but it does not have absolute claim. Only God is sovereign.

In his answer, Jesus did reject the Zealot concept of the kingdom of God as nationalistic. Jesus came to save mankind by bringing all under God's rule; he did not come to establish one nation above the others.

2. *The Resurrection* (20:27–40)

The Sadducees did not believe in the resurrection, and probably one of their stock stories designed to embarrass those who did was that of the woman who married seven brothers. According to Jewish marriage law (Deut. 25:5), if a man's brother died childless, he was to take his widow and raise up children to him. In their story, a woman married seven brothers in turn according to this law. In heaven, whose wife would she be?

Jesus taught that in heaven marriage would not pertain to the life of God's children. He did not say that we would become angels but that God's children would be like angels, at least in this respect. This is not to say that sex is evil, for it is God's creation. It is to say that its purpose is served in this life and that it does not pertain to the next. His chief argument for the resurrection was based upon the fact that God is the God of individuals, like Abraham, Isaac, and Jacob. God *is* their God; it is not just that God *was* their God. God is the God of living, so these are yet alive. God is the God of individual persons, and the survival of these persons is required. Therefore, eternal life is a certainty. Life after death is assured.

3. David's Son (20:41–44)

After being questioned by his opponents, Jesus countered with a question they had omitted. Is the Christ David's son or David's Lord? Jesus was the son of David, but he claimed also to be the Christ. Paradoxically, he is both David's son according to the flesh (1:27,32,69; 2:4; Rom. 1:3) and David's Lord as the Christ. Jesus did not answer the question in detail, for its purpose was to silence the dishonest opponents who sought, not guidance, but only charges to use against him in court.

IV. SCRIBES AND A WIDOW (20:45 to 21:4)

As Jesus continued his teaching in the Temple, he drew a sharp contrast between selfish scribes who "devour widows' houses" and a poor widow who gave all that she had.

In selfish exploitation, the scribes were willing to sacrifice a widow, depriving her of house and land. Out of her love, the poor widow was willing to sacrifice herself.

The scribes were the scholars who prided themselves as the interpreters of the Scriptures, yet they knew them poorly. Was it because they "used" the Scriptures instead of giving themselves to the Scriptures? Why are we ourselves now engaged in study of the Scriptures? Why do we not capture more of their real intention? John A. Bengel, in 1732, had a helpful word about studying the Bible: "Thy whole self apply to the text; the whole text apply to thyself." One must give himself to the Scriptures if they are to yield to him their richest treasures. Like a proud scribe, one may learn much about the Scriptures and yet not be changed basically in ways that matter most. The Bible is not a book to be "used." Its message is to be trusted, cherished, and followed.

V. The Destruction of Jerusalem Again Foretold (21 : 5– 38)

Once more Jesus warned his disciples about the coming destruction of Jerusalem. Although the city's doom was made emphatic, that was not the main point. Jesus was pointing, not only to Jerusalem's fall, but also beyond it. The great assurance Jesus gave was that there is redemption and meaningful life beyond the destruction of the Temple and Jerusalem! Not one stone upon another would be left to Jerusalem, but this was not the end of the world (21:9). Precisely when all men's securities seem to be shaken, then one may "look up," and in lifting up his head see "redemption draw nigh" (21:28).

In this great eschatological discourse (discussion of "last things"), Jesus clearly predicted the destruction of Jerusalem and its Temple in A.D. 70. In A.D. 66, the Jews revolted against Rome, and only after a long and terrible siege did the city fall. The hopes of the people were kept alive through the siege by the assurance that the Messiah would come in time to save Jerusalem from the pagans. This understanding of Messiah as political and his employment of military force in establishing the kingdom of God was false, and faith in that kind of messianism was fatal to the nation. It was against such messianic hopes and messianic wars that Jesus warned his people (21:8–9).

The Temple upon which the disciples looked with such awe was the third and final Jewish Temple to be erected on Mount Moriah in Jerusalem. Construction of this Temple was begun under Herod the Great about 20 B.C., and it may not have been completed at the time of its destruction in A.D. 70. It consisted of several courts and buildings covering a thirteen-acre site. The Temple was built of massive white stones and was ornamented with gold and many costly stones and tapestries. It was considered to be one of the wonders of the ancient world.

More important than the magnificence of the Temple was the spiritual significance ascribed to it by the Jews. To many, it was the holiest place of all—the place most sanctified by God's presence. They believed that it could not be destroyed, for God would make it secure against all attacks. Jesus warned that the Temple would be destroyed. His greater concern was to assure his disciples that the destiny of his people and the future of his kingdom were not bound up with the Temple. When the things which can be shaken and destroyed are gone, that which he came to build would yet stand.

Much of Luke 21:5–33 clearly has to do with the destruction of Jerusalem. (Although Luke probably wrote after A.D. 70, there is no reason why Jesus could not have anticipated the destruction of Jerusalem. The Jews and Romans were on a "collision course" long before A.D. 70; and Jerusalem, as a mountain city, would have to be taken by siege.) Verse 20 is explicit about armies surrounding the city; it was fulfilled

in the war of A.D. 66–70. What is said about fleeing to the
mountains (v. 21) and the special suffering of mothers with
infants and small children has meaning with respect to war,
but flight would be irrelevant to the end of the world. This
is not to deny that the passage has overtones which refer
to the coming of the Son of man at the end of the world.
Luke's Gospel does see the world as under God, moving
toward a goal in both judgment and redemption. The destruction of Jerusalem does foreshadow the greater judgment
which shall come upon the whole world at the end of history.
But the immediate concern of Jesus was to turn his people
from false and vain hopes to a true hope. He sought to turn
them from faith in some political messiah who would promise a restored national Israel, thought of as the kingdom of
God.

Redemption is not bound up with Jerusalem, its Temple,
or the nation of Israel. This is the great assurance of Jesus'
discourse.

Jesus instructed his disciples in what they were to turn
to as well as turn *from*. They were not to be led astray by
false messiahs and messianic wars (21:8–9). They were to
bear their witness in the face of rejection and persecution,
with the assurance of God's help in their suffering for the
gospel (21:10–19). Much figurative language is employed,
to be taken seriously but not in every case literally; for example, "Some of you they shall cause to be put to death
. . . and not a hair of your head shall perish" (21:16–18).
Some would be martyred, but even in martyrdom there
would be no ultimate loss to the follower of Christ. The
disciples' business is to avoid the kind of life that can only
end in "nausea [surfeiting], drunkenness, and the distrac-
tions of life" (v. 34). The disciple is to bear the witness of
a triumphant life (vv. 12–19), and watch for the Son of
man's triumphant coming (v. 36).

10

Jesus' Death and Resurrection

22:1 to 24:53

THE STORY OF the death and resurrection of Jesus dominates
each of the four Gospels, even as the death and resurrection
belonged to the heart of early Christian faith and preaching. Paul did not speak for himself alone in saying, "Far be
it from me to glory except in the cross of our Lord Jesus
Christ" (Gal. 6:14, RSV); and "If Christ has not been raised
from the dead, then is our preaching empty and your faith
also is empty" (1 Cor. 15:14). Without the resurrection of
Christ, there is little likelihood that a movement would have
survived the death of Jesus. The death itself came as a shock
to his closest disciples, for their messianic understandings
were such that they did not believe that he could suffer
death. They did not expect him to die; and when he was
crucified, they did not expect to see him alive again.

The earliest Christians were compelled to rethink the
death of Jesus. It was a "stumblingblock" to Jews and "fool-
ishness" to Gentiles (1 Cor. 1:23). That is, it contradicted
Jewish concepts of the Messiah and caused them to stumble
at the claims made for him. The cross meant only weakness
and defeat to Gentiles, and the suggestion that the way of
the cross was to be esteemed was to them a foolish joke.
By all worldly standards, the death of Jesus was a colossal
failure. Only in the light of the resurrection were the disciples
able to reassess the death of Jesus. In the light of the resurrection and by reading again their Scriptures, they were

able to see the cross as God's power and God's wisdom (1 Cor. 1:24). This became the heart of the earliest preaching, in which was shown historically how the death of Jesus was brought about and theologically what it meant. The Gospels are in one sense an expansion of this preaching, each moving to the death and resurrection as its climax.

Luke recorded early hints of the fate which awaited Jesus (2:35; 4:24); and, from chapter 9 (vv. 22,31,44,51) on, he gave repeated reminders that the shadow of the cross had fallen across the path of Jesus. The death is presented as a bitter cup from which Jesus shrank, but which he drank (22:42). Luke demonstrated the innocence of Jesus: as acknowledged in his trials before Pilate (23:13–14) and Herod Antipas (23:15); and as recognized by one of the thieves crucified with him (23:41), by the centurion who carried out the execution (23:47), by the multitudes (23:48), and by Joseph of Arimathea (23:50–53).

Writing in a time when Christianity was moving deeper into the Roman world, Luke was deeply concerned to demonstrate that Jesus was not a seditionist who had encouraged rebellion against the Empire. Romans would normally understand messianic and kingdom talk as political. The fact that Jesus was crucified under the Roman governor Pilate would itself call for explanation in later times. The charges that had been made against Jesus were basically political: "We found this man subverting our nation and forbidding tribute to Caesar, and saying himself to be Christ, a king" (23:2). These were not the real grievances which the Pharisees, at least, had against Jesus; but these were political charges which they found most suited to their purposes.

Luke's interest was not simply to protect Christians against the false charge of sedition. He was much more concerned to show that Jesus had not come to settle Israel's dispute with Rome. Jesus was not a mere national deliverer. He had come as "a light for revelation to the Gentiles" as well as for the glory of Israel (2:32). He had come not to "restore the kingdom to Israel" (Acts 1:6), but that "repentance and forgiveness of sins should be preached in his name unto all the nations—beginning at Jerusalem" (24:47).

I. THE LAST SUPPER (22:1–23)

There are four accounts of the Last Supper in the New Testament (Matt. 26:17–30; Mark 14:12–26; Luke 22:1–23; 1 Cor. 11:17–34). The fact of multiple accounts, along with the care with which Jesus planned the Supper and the evidences of frequent observance in the early church, indicate the primary importance of the Supper to Jesus and the early church. Jesus' careful planning of the Supper is reflected in the fact that a large upper room had been prepared and reserved for the purpose (22:12). To avoid interference, the location was kept secret; the disciples were to be guided to it by a man bearing a pitcher of water (normally a woman's task). The importance of the Supper to Jesus is reflected in his saying, "With desire I desired to eat this passover with you before I suffer" (22:15). What is the meaning of the Lord's Supper, instituted on the night of the Last Supper?

The Lord's Supper unmistakably is a memorial of remembering of Jesus, with special reference to his death. But is that all? Possibly the Lord's Supper means less than it ought to many Christians today because its rich New Testament meaning has been reduced to that of a memorial. The Lord's Supper not only looks back in gratitude to God for what he accomplished at Golgotha; it looks ahead to the coming of the Lord Jesus in the fulness of his kingdom. In the Passover observance, the Jews looked back to their deliverance from Egyptian bondage; but they also looked ahead to a new deliverance by the expected Messiah. The Lord's Supper is likewise a memory and a hope; it is thanksgiving and expectation. In 1 Corinthians 10:16, the Supper is "the communion of the blood of Christ" and "the communion of the body of Christ" (KJV). The Greek word for "communion" is *koinonia*. A meaningful observance of the Supper is one in which Christians engage together with Christ and with one another in an act of fellowship, grateful remembrance, confident hope, renewal of covenant, and thanksgiving to God.

Jesus employed as symbols ordinary things from the table—a loaf of bread and a cup of wine. The loaf and the cup are of themselves symbols. The loaf symbolizes his body. The cup is itself a symbol of the blood or the life poured out for us and of which we partake. Although the Lord's Supper employs symbols—the loaf and the cup—its meaningful observance is more than a symbol. Remembrance, hope, thanksgiving, fellowship, and proclamation are not symbols. The presence of the Spirit of the living Christ is not a symbol; it is real! So, the Supper employs symbols, but far more than symbolism is involved in meaningful observance of the Supper.[1]

An obvious problem confronts the reader in Luke's account of the Last Supper, for he introduces "a cup" (22:17), "a loaf" (22:19), and again "the cup" (22:20). Were there two cups, one before and one following the bread? In the Passover, four cups of wine were served; and possibly this forms the background to the two cups in Luke's account. In one reference, Paul speaks of the cup and then the loaf (1 Cor. 10:16), and in another of the loaf then the cup (1 Cor. 11:23,25). The details concerning the sequence of the Supper events are elusive and not of primary importance.

More important than the order of the bread and the cup is the original text concerning the loaf. (Some old manuscripts in Greek, Latin, and Syriac omit Luke 22:19b–20. This is a difficult problem not pursued here.) In oldest

---

[1] For an extended discussion of the Lord's Supper by this writer, see his *New Testament Theology*, pp. 235-249.

manuscripts (handwritten Bibles before the invention of printing), Paul's account reads, "This is my body for you" (1 Cor. 11:24). This agrees with the account in the Gospels. Jesus did not say "broken for you." That is a late reading, added by copyists who misunderstood Jesus' statement. John's Gospel declares, "A bone of him shall not be broken" (19:36). The real importance in correcting the reading at this point is that "broken" reverses one meaning of the Supper. Partaking of one loaf and drinking of one cup symbolizes the oneness of the church in Christ: "Seeing that we the many are one loaf, one body; for we all partake of the one loaf" (1 Cor. 10:17). This is why the meaning of the Supper is contradicted when it is eaten in disunity.

II. ALONE IN THE MIDST OF MANY (22:24–65)

Proud contention about greatness among the twelve (22:24–30); an empty boast of a loyalty that failed (22:31–34); ears that heard not, confusing the weapons of darkness with those of light (22:35–38); a bitter cup while friends slept (22:39–46); betrayal by a kiss (22:47–53); denial by a frightened follower (22:54–62); and mocking and buffeting at the hands of coarse buffoons—these were among the sorrows endured by "the Man of Sorrows."

How can one comment on all of that? The judgment runs deep. Jesus was betrayed not just by the world but also by his own. Possibly all we can do is read this story of man's shame and bow our heads, for it is the story of our shame too. In one sense, we were not there; yet in another sense, we were there. Our kind of sins were there. Jesus was misunderstood, betrayed, denied, abandoned, and finally crucified by our kind of people. Pride, selfish ambition, fear, insensitivity to the light he brings, and all the other sins of that night long ago may be found in us, too.

Who among us does not measure greatness by the world's false standards (22:24–30)? Who among us does not boast of loyalty which he fails to make good, often, like Simon, betraying those whom we love most dearly (22:31–34)? Who of us has not listened to Christ say, "Sell your cloak and buy a sword" only to understand in terms of the literal, missing the deeper meaning (22:35–38)? Who of us has not slept through Gethsemane, leaving the bitter cup to him alone (22:39–46)? Who of us has not, like Judas, betrayed the Master with an empty kiss, or with lip service when he called for life (22:47–53)?

A few verses in this section call for explanation. The kingdom which Jesus appoints his followers (22:29) is one of sovereignty through service. The only greatness offered is that of humble service. When Jesus said, "It is enough" to his dull disciples, he did not mean that the two swords they showed him were enough. He refused the use of even one sword. "It is enough" is an expression meaning, "Enough of that!" They had missed the point about selling one's cloak to buy a sword. He used "sword" as a symbol for power. He meant that his disciples were entering upon a life which would demand all the resources at their command. It was no easy life to which he had called them—not one for the timid and weak. They would need to be armed with courage and determination so they would not give up the struggle. Instead, they understood "sword" in a literal sense. In effect, Jesus said, "Skip it!"

III. THE TRIAL OF JESUS (22:66 to 23:25)

1. Before the Sanhedrin (22:66–71)

The Sanhedrin was the supreme court of the Jews, a body of about seventy Sadducees and Pharisees presided over by the high priest. It seems that this court did not have the power of capital punishment, this being reserved by the Romans to their own courts. Accordingly, the Sanhedrin could not sentence Jesus to death. Its strategy was to gather evidence and formulate charges which would interest a Roman court.

When the Sanhedrin asked Jesus if he were the Christ, a term was employed which meant different things to different people. To the Romans, "Christ" would have political overtones. Jesus exposed the closed minds of his opponents in saying, "If I tell you, you will not believe" (26:67). Theirs were ears that refused to hear and eyes which refused to see.

Jesus substituted the term "Son of man" for their term "Christ" (22:69). The term "Son of man" was freer from confusion with political ideas. The Son of man receives the kingdom from God alone, not from man. It was a more inclusive term, designating one who was from heaven and whose role it was to establish a kingdom which was universal and eternal. Jesus saw his kinship to be with humanity and not with Israel alone. He had come to bring all nations under God's rule, not to create a kingdom of Israel.

To the question about his claim to be "the Son of God," Jesus answered, "You are the ones saying that I am" (22:70). In effect, Jesus was accepting the title. However, he drove home the point that they were the ones who had used the term. In a sense, they were recognizing him in the very act of denying him. Judgment was brought upon them because they recognized him yet did not acknowledge him.

2. Before Pilate and Herod Antipas (23:1–23)

The charges made against Jesus as he was sent to Pilate were political: "subverting the nation"; "forbidding tribute to Caesar"; and calling himself "Christ, a king." In effect, Jesus was being accused of treason—a rebel against the Roman authority. Jesus had consistently rejected this very role, for the popular conception of Messiah was political. Ironically, Jesus was falsely sentenced for the very thing from which he tried in vain to turn his people. When Pilate asked Jesus if he were king of the Jews, Jesus replied, "You are saying it." The statement was Pilate's, not his own. The reply could be punctuated as a question. (The old manuscripts have no punctuation, not even spacing between words.) Possibly Jesus asked, "Are you saying this?" Jesus' answer would be both yes and no. He was a king, but not in the sense in which a Roman would understand it.

Herod Antipas, ruler over Galilee, was in Jerusalem for the Feast of the Passover; so Pilate sent Jesus to him. Pilate may have sought thereby both to flatter Herod and to seek some relief from the pressure put upon him by the Sanhedrin. Herod's curiosity about Jesus was not matched by any serious inquiry. Jesus had nothing to say to this royal buffoon who mocked Jesus and returned him to Pilate.

Luke was careful to bring out the fact that neither Pilate nor Herod found Jesus guilty (23:13–15). Pilate made some attempt to free Jesus, but never did he put truth and right before expediency. He probably had just enough sense of justice to shrink back from sacrificing an innocent man. Moreover, he probably resented being pushed around by the religious leaders. He offered to release Jesus, but they asked for Barabbas—a Jewish insurrectionist against Rome.

Many scholars today insist that New Testament writers have distorted the record, shifting blame for the death of Jesus from the Romans to the Jews. In part, this is an effort to counter the anti-Semitism which has been the shame of much of the Western world. It is well to rebuke such anti-Semitism; it is indefensible to charge New Testament writers with thus distorting history. Paul was not anti-Semitic, yet he wrote in what is possibly his earliest extant letter, "the Jews . . . killed the Lord Jesus" (1 Thess. 2:14–15). That Jewish people in the first century helped crucify Jesus does not incriminate Jews today any more than non-Jews. The judgment for this sin rightly falls upon the whole human race, not upon any one nation alone. The proper question for each person today is, "What will I do with Jesus?"

IV. THE DEATH AND BURIAL OF JESUS (23:26–56)

Even as he approached the cross, Jesus had more thought for others than for himself. As the women lamented him, he said, "Daughters of Jerusalem, weep not for me, but weep for yourselves, and for your children" (23:28). He seems to have been thinking in particular of the fate which was soon to come upon Jerusalem and the nation.

Verse 31 is a puzzle: "For if they do these things in a green tree, what shall be done in the dry?" Probably he meant that if a Roman governor would sacrifice a man whom he knew to be innocent of charges of rebellion, they could expect much worse should the nation indeed follow the course of rebellion. Even on his way to death, Jesus called the nation to repentance. The slaughter of the people and the burning of Jerusalem in A.D. 70 vindicated the words of Jesus.

The world's misunderstanding of Jesus and his cross is imbedded in the scoffing remark, "Others he saved; let him save himself, if this one is the Christ of God, the elect" (23:35). This misses the basic truth of the gospel. To seek to save oneself is to destroy oneself. Only in losing self to God may one be saved. Had Jesus turned from his mission to save others and sought to save himself, then all would have been lost. Had Jesus turned out to be like other men, bent upon saving themselves, he could have saved no one. It is precisely in his self-renunciation, his self-sacrifice, and self-giving that he proves to be the Saviour.

This is the deepest meaning of the cross. It is the reversal of Adam's way of self-trust, self-love, and self-assertion. The death of Jesus Christ becomes saving only as one is drawn into personal union with Christ so that he may "crucify" the old self-centered man and create the new Christ-centered man.

V. THE RISEN CHRIST (24:1–51)

Only the personal appearance of the risen Christ convinced anyone that he was alive. The empty tomb did not convince friend or foe. To the apostles, the report of Mary Magdalene, Joanna, Mary, the mother of James, and other women sounded like "idle talk" (24:11). Verse 12 is absent from most ancient manuscripts; but even as it stands, it does not ascribe more than wonder to Peter following his inspection of the empty tomb. The faith of the early church did not rest upon the negative evidence of an empty tomb, but upon the positive evidence of the living Lord who appeared to many.

Two men of Emmaus reflected the feelings and thinking of many as they walked home from Jerusalem. They did not recognize Jesus as he joined them along the way. When Jesus asked what they were talking about, they showed surprise that one would think there was anything else to talk about except the events of the past few days. The popular understanding of the role of Messiah, as well as their keen disappointment, came out as they said: "But we hoped that it was he who should redeem Israel" (24:21). The basic idea in "redeem" is to liberate. It was expected that Messiah would liberate Israel from Roman bondage and restore the kingdom of Israel (Acts 1:6). The crucifixion of Jesus was seen as fatal to the hope that he would prove to be the Christ.

From the Jewish Scriptures, referred to as "Moses and the prophets" and in their threefold division as "Moses and the prophets and the psalms" (24:27,44), Jesus interpreted to them the things concerning himself. He was the Christ, but not the political deliverer expected by much of Judaism. He explained that his work was to save people from their sins, not to save one nation from another. His concern was with the world: " . . . repentance and forgiveness of sins should be preached in his name unto all the nations, beginning from Jerusalem" (24:47).

Luke had a special interest in presenting Jesus as concerned for the whole world. What began at Jerusalem was designed for the world. What in Luke's day had reached out into the world and included the Gentiles had begun in Jerusalem. It was no accident or miscarriage of divine plan; rather it was the accomplishment of Christ's will that the door of faith was opened to all people.

It is significant that Jesus opened the Scriptures to men's minds (24:32), and he opened their minds to the Scriptures (24:45). An open Bible and open minds resulted in "burning hearts" (24:32). The purpose of the Scriptures is reflected in verse 27, where it is said that from the Scriptures Jesus interpreted to the men of Emmaus the things concerning himself. The Bible is "witness to Christ." If it does not lead to faith in Christ, its basic purpose has been missed. Its purpose is first to lead to discipleship and next to instruct in discipleship. Precious book though it be, it is not an end in itself. It points beyond itself to Christ and to the world which he came to save.

VI. THE DISCIPLES CONTINUING IN JERUSALEM (24:50–53)

Following the ascension of Christ, the disciples "returned to Jerusalem with great joy and were continually in the Temple, blessing God." It is clear that Luke's message is not complete at this point. The book of Acts is the second volume to Luke-Acts. The two books are projected as one work in two parts. In Acts is traced out the struggle for an unfettered gospel, a gospel to be preached unhindered to Jew, Samaritan, and Gentile.

The Gospel of Luke closes with the disciples joyfully residing in Jerusalem. Acts closes with a picture of Paul in Rome, preaching "unhindered" to any who would hear the gospel, Jew or Gentile. In the two volumes, Luke shows that Christianity was born within Judaism; and its Jewish followers lived joyfully for a time in Jerusalem and worshiped in the Temple. The Gentile church which emerged came from truest Judaism. This breakthrough was of God. But sad and tragic was the self-exclusion of the Jews from the church which, through much pain, finally rose above the distinctions of nationality and race.

It is hazardous to try to sum up the message of Luke's Gospel, but some of its basic concerns are clear. Luke's stated purpose was to draw up a narrative which would give certainty to the things in which Theophilus had been instructed (1:1–4). He presented Jesus in terms of his divine and human origin, in terms of his teaching and his mighty works, and in terms of his triumphant death and resurrection. Luke's special purpose in his Gospel seems to have been to show how Jesus offered himself to all people, with a concern to meet all their needs, and how he was gradually thrust out by his own family and nation. In Acts, Luke showed that the gospel is to be preached indiscriminately to all nations and that the church, as it overcame barriers of nationality and race, was gradually thrust out of the Temple and synagogues. It cost Jesus his life to offer himself to all people. It cost the church its original home to open its doors to all people. The gospel is indeed "bitter and sweet" (Rev. 10:10). It is free and yet costs everything. Christ gives all and demands all. It is to such a Lord and Saviour that we are called.

Epilogue

In LUKE-ACTS is traced the early struggle for an unhindered gospel. As is true for any freedom, the victory for an unhindered gospel is never won once for all. This is an unending struggle, to be fought through to victory in each generation, in each community, and in each individual life. What hindrances threaten the gospel today? Could it be provincialism, whether geographical, cultural, religious, or otherwise? Could it be racial prejudice and discrimination? Could it be the denial of grace by the substitution of human "merit," whether of the advantages of birth, creedal orthodoxy, ritual excellence, or whatever we hold up to God of our own which we think sufficient to lift us above other people? Who are our despised "Samaritans" or "Gentiles" or "publicans" or "sinners"? What are our counterparts to ritual washing of hands, days of fasting, circumcision, and sabbath observance? By what superficial things do we lift ourselves above people about us, excluding them, and thus excluding ourselves from him who ate with publican and sinners? What barriers do we place before the gospel which is intended for all people?

Suggested Audiovisual Materials

A filmstrip (50 frames, color, recording) has been prepared specifically for use in connection with the study of *Studies in Luke's Gospel*. It will be effective to show this filmstrip at some time prior to the first class period. Produced by Broadman Films, *Luke's Gospel* is available from your Baptist Book Store.

Other projected aids will prove valuable as extracurricular materials. Selected frames may be used as interest centers. (See suggestions in the *Teaching Guide for Studies in Luke's Gospel* by Zimmer, which is available from your Baptist Book Store.)

Chapter 1

FILMSTRIPS: *Luke's Gospel,* 50 frames, color, recording; *The Gospel According to Luke,* 42 frames, color, recording; *The Four Gospels,* 37 frames, color, recording

Chapter 2

FILMSTRIPS: *The Birth of John,* 20 frames, color; *The Birth of John the Baptist,* 20 minutes, color; *Unto Us a Saviour,* 50 frames, color, recording; *The Presentation,* 28 frames, color, recording
SLIDES: Cc 549, *The Boy Christ in the Temple—Clementz;* Cc 130, *Christ Among the Doctors*
MOTION PICTURES: *Birth of the Saviour,* 14 minutes, color; *Childhood of Jesus,* 14 minutes, color

Chapter 3

FILMSTRIPS: *The Ministry of John the Baptist,* 30 frames, color; *Jesus Begins His Ministry,* 26 frames, color

Chapter 4

FILMSTRIPS: *Jesus' First Tour of Galilee,* 25 frames, color; *Rejection at Nazareth,* 30 frames, color, recording
MOTION PICTURES: *Jesus at Nazareth and Capernaum,* 14 minutes, color; *Jesus, Lord of the Sabbath,* 14 minutes, color
SLIDE: N145 *Jesus in the Synagogue of Nazareth*

Chapter 5

FILMSTRIPS: *Jesus Performs Miracles in Galilee*, 23 frames, color; *The Centurion's Servant*, 34 frames, color, recording
MOTION PICTURES: *The Greater Guilt*, 28 minutes; *I Am the Resurrection*, 19 minutes, color

Chapter 6

FILMSTRIP: *The Good Samaritan*, 19 frames, color
MOTION PICTURES: *Before Abraham Was, I Am*, 19 minutes, color, *Road to Jericho*, 30 minutes

Chapter 7

MOTION PICTURES: *Rich Fool*, 28 minutes; *This Night*, 28 minutes

Chapter 8

FILMSTRIP: *The Prodigal Son*, 18 frames, color
MOTION PICTURE: *This My Son*, 29 minutes
SLIDES: Cc 401, *The Lost Sheep—Soord;* Ha 768, *The Prodigal Son Leaving Home;* N 180, *The Prodigal's Awakening;* N 181, *The Prodigal's Return*

Chapter 9

FILMSTRIP: *Triumphal Entry and Cleansing of the Temple*, 44 frames, color, recording
SLIDE: Cc 776, *Triumphal Entry into Jerusalem—Plockhorst*
MOTION PICTURE: *Last Journey to Jerusalem*, 19 minutes, color

Chapter 10

FILMSTRIPS: *The Last Supper*, 28 frames, color; *The Upper Room*, 30 frames, color, recording; *The Passover Supper and Betrayal*, 30 frames, color, recording; *He Is Risen*, 45 frames, color, recording; *Jesus' Resurrection*, 21 frames, color; *The Resurrection*, 31 frames, color, recording; *The Resurrection Story*, 25 frames, color
SLIDES: Cc 670, *The Last Supper—Leonardo da Vinci;* Ha 301, *The Last Supper—Wood;* Cm 142, *The Lord's Supper—Sallman;* Cc 133, *Christ in Gethsemane—Hofmann;* Ch 275, *Crucifixion—Munkasy;* Cc 56, *The Crucifixion—Clementz*
MOTION PICTURES: *The Upper Room*, 14 minutes, color; *Betrayal in Gethsemane*, 15 minutes, color; *Jesus Before the High Priest*, 15 minutes, color; *The Crucifixion*, 20 minutes, color; *The Lord Is Risen*, 15 minutes, color

Bibliography*

Arndt, William F. *Bible Commentary: Gospel of St. Luke*. St. Louis, Missouri: Concordia Publishing House, 1956.

Barclay, William. *The Gospel of Luke*. Philadelphia: Westminster Press, 1956.

Browning, W. R. F. *The Gospel According to Saint Luke*. New York: Collier Books, 1962.

Carter, John Franklin. *A Layman's Harmony of the Gospels*. Nashville: Broadman Press, 1961.

Edersheim, Alfred. *Jesus the Messiah* (abridged edition of *The Life and Times of Jesus the Messiah*). Grand Rapids: Eerdmans Publishing Company, 1954.

Edge, Findley. *A Quest for Vitality in Religion*. Nashville: Broadman Press, 1963.

Erdman, Charles Rosenbury. *The Gospel of Luke*. Philadelphia: Westminster Press, 1921.

Geldenhuys, Norval. *Commentary on the Gospel of Luke*. Grand Rapids: Eerdmans Publishing Company, 1952.

Hobbs, Herschel H. *Exposition of the Gospel of Luke*. Grand Rapids: Baker Book House, 1966.

Manson, William. *The Gospel of Luke*. New York: Harper & Row, 1930.

Miller, Donald George. *Gospel According to Luke*. Richmond: John Knox Press, 1959.

Morgan, George Campbell. *The Gospel According to Luke*. Westwood, New Jersey: Fleming H. Revell Company, 1931.

Stagg, Frank. *New Testament Theology*. Nashville: Broadman Press, 1962.

Tinsley, E. J. *The Gospel According to Luke*. Cambridge: The University Press, 1965.

Trueblood, Elton. *The Company of the Committed*. New York: Harper & Row, 1961.

Turlington, Henry E. *Luke's Witness to Jesus*. Nashville: Broadman Press, 1967.

Ward, Wayne. *The Drama of Redemption*. Nashville: Broadman Press, 1966.

---

* The listing of these books does not imply endorsement of their total contents by author or publishers of *Studies in Luke's Gospel*.

141

Helps for the Teacher

Preparation should involve a careful reading of Luke's Gospel in at least two translations. Then read the study course book you have in hand. Probably you will want to use other reference books of your own or some from the list on pages xi-xii.

Preparation of Materials

You will need maps, posters, newsprint, and audiovisual equipment and materials. You will want to collect reference materials and have them at hand when you make assignments to class members, and perhaps you will want to use them for on-the-spot research to find answers to spontaneous questions. You would do well to keep paper and pencil handy as you go through the study course book. Jot down posters needed, assignments to be made, possible uses of audiovisuals, objects which might be used to drive home a lesson, and so on. Such a list made and used in preparation will give you a sense of readiness when it is time to teach the class.

Methods

Perhaps you would like to use other persons to help you in various ways with your class sessions. Such involvement on the part of a number of persons will stimulate interest and offer variety for the study. You might consider such group learning methods as panels, panel-forum, small study groups, group discussions, role play, brainstorming, research, Scripture searching, listening teams, and symposiums. For a helpful discussion of these learning methods, see *A Primer for Teachers and Leaders* by LeRoy Ford, Nashville: Broadman Press, 1963.

Schedule

It would be impossible in the six hours required for this study to do anything more than survey the Gospel of Luke. Therefore, you might consider using focal passages selected to highlight the outline and development of Luke's Gospel. Such selectivity will help you to allocate time appropriately and will assure that your class will get a balanced study of the Gospel.

Assuming that you will devote at least six hours to this course, you might organize your study into eight forty-five minute sessions as follows:

Session 1—Part 1, chapter 1
    Focal passage: Luke 1:1–4
Session 2—Part 2, chapters 2 and 3
    Focal passages: Luke 1:5–13,26–35,39–42,51–80; 2:1–14,22,25–35,41–52; 4:1–13
Session 3—Part 3, chapter 4
    Focal passages: Luke 4:14–30,31–37; 5:12–15
Session 4—chapter 5
    Focal passages: Luke 6:12–16,27–36,37–38; 7:1–17; 8:1–18; 9:18–36
Session 5—Part 4, chapters 6 and 7
    Focal passages: Luke 9:51–56; 10:1–12,25–37; 11:14–23; 12:1–7,13–32,35–48; 14:25–35
Session 6—chapter 8
    Focal passages: Luke 15:3–32; 16:1–31; 17:1–19
Session 7—Part 5, chapter 9
    Focal passages: Luke 19:28–46; 19:47 to 20:18; 21:5–38
Session 8—chapter 10
    Focal passages: Luke 22:7–23,39–48; 23:1,13–26,32–49; 24:50–53

Special Helps

The focal passage approach outlined above has been used in compiling a workbook for use in a study of Luke's Gospel. Available from Baptist Book Stores, the workbook is 8½ x 11 inches and is punched for three ring binder. It contains study questions and the printed focal passages from the American Bible Society's new translation, *The New Testament in Today's English Version*. Wide margins alongside the text encourage the student to make notes from his personal study and during class discussions. Sections of the workbook may be used as assignments for makeup work. The entire book may be used for home study in the place of questions appearing on pages 146-48 of this book.

Session by session teaching suggestions are also available. The teacher would benefit from a consideration of these detailed suggestions which appear in the *Teaching Guide for Studies in Luke's Gospel*, by Dwayne Zimmer. Copies may be obtained from Baptist Book Stores.

Promotion

Preparation of class members is good promotion. Your class sessions will be more meaningful if members of the class are prepared. Plan to distribute study course books a week before the class meets. Encourage the congregation to begin reading Luke's Gospel and the study course book. It would be helpful to show the filmstrip *Luke's Gospel* in preparation for the class on Luke's Gospel. Perhaps you would want to suggest that as members view the filmstrip and as they read from the Bible they make questions which they would like to have answered about Luke and his writing. These could be turned in to you at the beginning of the course and be used to create interest each session.

Ask someone in the congregation to prepare posters announcing the study of *Luke's Gospel*.

Preenrolment is also good promotion. Consider distributing enrolment cards along with the study course books a week prior to beginning classes.

A Possible Teaching Plan

You will note above the suggestion that you use a focal passage approach in surveying the Gospel. This will preclude the verse-by-verse approach. A sample lesson plan is given below. Perhaps it will be suggestive of further plans that you might make for each session. (For more complete plans, see *Teaching Guide for Studies in Luke's Gospel* by Dwayne Zimmer, available from your Baptist Book Store.)

1. Begin session for chapter 2 with the singing of several Christmas hymns, one verse each. Lead in prayer of thanksgiving for the coming of Christ into the world.

2. Be sure the group understands that the major thrust of this session is that Christianity had its origin within the faith of Israel, in genuine Jewish piety. During this period, seek to show the relationship between Judaism and Christianity and to help your class gain a new appreciation for Jewish origins.

3. Use a symposium to present the contents of chapter 2. Assign the topics well in advance and ask the participants to confine their discussion to the main ideas of (1) God's initiative behind each event, and (2) the strong Jewish backgrounds revealed by Luke in these beginnings. Topics are given below:

(1) The Birth of John—Luke 1:5–25,57–80; and sections I. 1. and II. 1. of the study course book.

(2) The Birth of Jesus—Luke 1:26–38; 2:1–20; Matthew 1:18–25; and sections I. 2. and II. 2. of study course book.

(3) Mary's Visit with Elizabeth—Luke 1:29–56; and sections I. 3. of study course book.

(4) Relationship of Simeon and Anna to Jesus—Luke 2:1–40; and section III. 1. of book.

(5) The Awareness of Jesus Concerning His Relationship with Earthly Parents and Heavenly Father—Luke 2:41–52; and section III. 2. of the book.

Use questions below to summarize the study. (These questions are taken from the workbook, which is also available at Baptist Book Stores.)

1. Who are the main characters in Luke 1:5–13?

2. Luke depicted the beginnings of Christianity in _____
   _____ _____ .

3. What phrase in 2:78 means messianic redemption?

4. What proof appears in 2:1–14 that Luke's emphasis is on a "gospel for all people"?

5. Why was Jesus brought to Jerusalem? What offering was made? What was Simeon waiting to see? What was Simeon's prophesy?

For Review and Written Work

The answers to the following questions may be found by a close reading of each chapter of the study course book.

PART 1 AND CHAPTER 1 (fill in blanks):

1. The Gospel of Luke will be studied in _____ parts.
2. The parts are:

   _____ (title) _____ (reference)

   _____   _____

   _____   _____

   _____   _____

   _____   _____

3. Luke's purpose and message were meant to: _____
   _____; to present an _____ _____;
   and to trace the emergence of a _____ _____.
4. When Luke wrote, the barrier hardest to cross with the gospel
   was the _____ between _____ and _____.
5. Christianity was born within truest _____.

PART 2 AND CHAPTER 2:

6. List at least four things with which this part of the book is
   concerned.
7. List the two announcements discussed in this chapter.
8. Identify: Elizabeth, Zacharias, Anna, Simeon.

CHAPTER 3 (Write T by true statements, F by false. Check your
answers by Dr. Stagg's material.)

9. _____ Repentance in New Testament usage means only
   "change of mind."
10. _____ John's preaching was bound up with judgment upon
    sins.
11. _____ Jesus' followers quickly grasped the idea of a suffer-
    ing Messiah.
12. _____ Luke traced the lineage of Jesus back to Adam
    through Joseph.
13. _____ Luke and Matthew have identical genealogies.
14. _____ All three temptations of Jesus were messianic in
    nature.

146

CHAPTER 4:

15. Write a brief paragraph on the basic conflicts between Jesus and the Pharisees.

CHAPTER 5 (Match a statement or word on left with an item on right.)

16. _____ unable to heal
17. _____ non-Jews
18. _____ love
19. _____ "good" and "corrupt"
20. _____ Jesus' concern
21. _____ John
22. _____ feeding of five thousand

a. publicans and sinners
b. not condition, but kind
c. lack of faith
d. of the old order
e. high point of Jesus' popularity
f. unselfishness
g. for all people

CHAPTER 6 (Complete the following statements.)

23. Luke 9:51 is significant in the life of Jesus because:
24. The instructions given to the seventy were:
25. To be able really to be a "good Samaritan," one must first:
26. Following are some of the signs Jesus gave and the rejection he received as recorded in this portion of Luke:

CHAPTER 7 (fill in blanks):

27. Discipleship offers freedom from _____, _____, and _____.
28. The kingdom of God was described by Jesus through the parables of the _____ _____ and _____.
29. Discipleship is finding a new way of life in rejecting the way of _____ - _____, _____ - _____, and _____ - _____.

CHAPTER 8 (discuss):

30. God's joy is seen in three parables. Write a brief statement on each parable and show where Dr. Stagg's emphasis gives new insight into these parables.
31. What does Dr. Stagg suggest is the *chief lesson* in the story of the rich man and Lazarus?
32. What are some of the assurances Jesus gave concerning the kingdom of God?
33. What is the paradox of which Dr. Stagg speaks in the last paragraph of this chapter?

CHAPTER 9 (fill in blanks):

34. Jesus' triumphal entry might better be termed the _____ _____.

35. The parable of the vineyard illustrates one main point: _____ _____ _____.

36. The scribes and chief priests attempted to trap Jesus through questions about _____ _____ _____ and about the _____.

37. In discussing the destruction of Jerusalem, the great assurance Jesus gives is that _____ _____.

CHAPTER 10 (discuss):

38. What is the real meaning of the death of Jesus? When does his death become saving for any person?

39. What does Dr. Stagg see as Luke's special purpose in his Gospel? in Acts?

40. Are there any barriers to the gospel today? If so, what are they?